D1732952

THE GOD THEY NEVER KNEW:
The Tragedy of Religion Without Relationship

THE GOD THEY NEVER KNEW:

The Tragedy of Religion Without Relationship

GEORGE OTIS, Jr.

REVISED EDITION

MOTT MEDIA

Leonard George Goss, Editor

Designed by Kurt Dietsch
Cover photo by Tim Bieber
Copy edited by Carolyn Stanford Goss, Leonard Goss and Ruth Schenk
Typeset by Professional Composition, Inc.

Manufactured in the United States of America

ISBN 0-915134-84-5

THIS BOOK IS DEDICATED TO:

WINKIE PRATNEY,
HARRY CONN
and
GORDON OLSON

WHO ENCOURAGED ME TO LOVE GOD WITH MY MIND
AS WELL.

I went into the sanctuary of God; then understood I their end.

Surely thou didst set them in slippery places: thou castedst them down into destruction.

How are they brought into desolation, as in a moment! they are utterly consumed with terrors. As a dream when one awaketh; so, O Lord, when thou awakest, thou shalt despise their image. Thus my heart was grieved . . . .

PSALM 73

TABLE OF CONTENTS

The Art of Building Your Own Cross
Seeing Eyes

FOREWORD

If the church of our Lord is to ever see revival in the true sense of the word, it must not be equated with evangelistic meetings. Rather, the truths explained in this book will need to be mastered and preached.

The writer has paid his "tuition" both academically and in practical service in the kingdom. Both of these are among the necessary ingredients of a worthwhile and profound author.

It seems to have never occurred to many speakers that if we are to love God with all of our heart, soul, mind and strength, He must have some lovable characteristics. In this book, George Otis, Jr. restores to our great God many of His true and lovable characteristics that various modern day theological concepts have obscured.

When God said in the first commandment, "Thou shalt have no other gods before Me," He didn't say, "Thou shalt not be an atheist." There are no atheists. Man is so created that he must have, and does have, a god. Perhaps his god is family, money, liquor, fame, health, education, beauty, power or security. These are just a few of the thousands of gods available to man. Every person has a "theology" and a god. The author is trying to get us to see, worship and serve the God of Abraham, Isaac and Jacob, maker of heaven and earth and father of our Lord Jesus Christ. Any other god will hurt not only ourselves, but those around us in a thousand ways.

George treats many important areas of theological thought in such a sound manner, that according to my knowledge, this book is a "must" for our time and people. His treatment of the atonement, wherein lies the real power of the gospel, is unparalleled in any other book on that subject today. His treatment of the "blood of Christ" removes it from the place of a new religious "rabbit's foot." This teaching may seem new to many readers, but it isn't. It is the same view of the atonement as preached by Charles G. Finney, Berge, Barnes, Luther, Wesley, N. W. Taylor and a host of others. It merits your attention, study and meditation.

Perhaps the most mispreached and ill-taught Bible verse of our day is Isaiah 55:9. The explanation of that verse in this book is a classic gem. The removal of "holiness" from the realm of the mystical and abstract to a learned and possible state has been long overdue. The author removes "faith" as an act or state of reaching out and embracing what you don't understand from the realm of magic. The emphasis on salvation as a right relationship or reality (instead of a technicality) is just exactly that which the blessed Holy Spirit can use to bring revival. The "forgotten doctrines," repentance and sin, are treated in an irenic way and not neglected. Repentance is not portrayed as being optional or subsequent to salvation.

Never has there been a book more timely and needed. Yet the biggest problem most will have with this material is that they will be forced to make up their minds as to whether they want to be "right" in a revivaless age, or embrace and preach these truths and see God's Holy Spirit lend credence to their propagation.

God has said, "Come, let us reason together." This book is for the person who dares to think. It is my prayer that millions will accept the challenge of God through this book.

Harry Conn
Rockford, Illinois

Author's Preface to the Second Edition

An author so fortunate to compose prefatory remarks for a second edition of his or her work finds it eminently easier the second time around. The reason for this, at least in my case, is the benefit of hindsight. The author knows what the public thought of the original effort, and is thus able to reconstruct weak points while reiterating the strong ones.

If the scores of positive letters and personal encounters over the past couple of years show the broader impact of *The God They Never Knew*, it is encouraging evidence indeed. Not, to be sure, that some strictly amateur literary effort has attracted some small acclaim, but rather that the kernels of truth so prayerfully sown within its covers produced such desirable effects in the lives of readers. This, when all is said and done, is what really matters. For in contrast to the fixation so many of us have with methodology and technique, God's emphasis is in *change*.

Perhaps some who saw the cover title of this book in its first format were surprised to find as they flipped through the pages that the book has very little to do with the spiritual ignorance of unreached peoples around the world. In this completely revised edition we have attempted to remove even the slightest confusion by changing the cover and adding a subtitle to better suit the book's primary thrust. *The God They Never Knew: The Tragedy of Religion Without Relationship*, as the new subtitle suggests, is concerned with the growing number of church(wo)men who indulge in formal religion without cultivating a personal relationship with the living Christ.

You may ask if such a thing is possible. Can one un-knowingly belong to one religion while under the impression that he or she is part of another? Rutgers Professor David Ehrenfeld analyzes this question in his book *The Arrogance of Humanism*. He answers, "If that person believes in the dogma of the former and only celebrates the latter, why not?" To whom else did Jesus direct His words in Matthew 7:21–23?

> Not every one who says to me, "Lord, Lord," will enter the kingdom of heaven; but he who does the will of my Father who is in heaven. Many will say to me on that day, "Lord, Lord, did we not prophesy in Your name, and in Your name cast out demons, and in Your name perform many miracles?" And then I will declare to them, *"I never knew you;* depart from Me, you who practice lawlessness.

What was their crime? Precisely that which killed Ananias and Sapphira—*they lied!* They did nothing in God's name; oh, it was on their lips, but they forgot that God looks on the heart, where He found other names. They wanted power without responsibility, and the name without the relationship.

That's what this book is all about—*a relationship.* In the chapters that follow, each of the major salvation doctrines are examined through the paradigm of this all important word. Those who look for a thorough, systematic theology will be disappointed, for that is not my purpose. Rather, we seek the Jesus the church has lost in its abstract, theological theorizing, "received by tradition from our fathers." The Jesus with whom we need a fresh and vital encounter.

Life is not a game we can play according to our own rules, for we are creatures. As creatures, we must seek our Source, recognizing that in spite for all our spiritual dialogue, service and fellowship, it is the relationship that counts. It is this relationship which must be cultivated at all costs. As C. S. Lewis put it, "We must starve eternally."

The world still echoes Pilate's class action question: "What is truth?" For there is an intuitive realization in the human heart that once it is found it will set us free. It remains my sincere hope that the truth in these pages will free you to worship God in a new dimension, as it has for me. It must be truth that unlocks the door of revelation, for there is no other key.

—George Otis, Jr.
Seattle, Washington
January, 1982

UNDERSTANDING

1/THE GOD THEY NEVER KNEW

> But they do not know the thoughts of the Lord,
> and they do not understand His purpose . . . .
> Micah 4:12 (NASB)

> The idolatrous heart assumes that God is other
> than He is—in itself a monstrous sin—and substi-
> tutes for the true God one made after its own like-
> ness.
> A. W. Tozer

> The only possible religion for twentieth-century
> man is a mystical religion and all theological lan-
> guage must be recognized as a language of sym-
> bols.
> F. C. Happold

It has been said that the process of getting to know another person—and even the process of falling in love—depends, to a considerable extent, on listening to what the other person says and asking questions to find out what he feels and thinks. Christianity is in its naked essence a relationship. Accordingly, you would be inclined to think that this type of interpersonal exploration and discovery would be a natural pursuit of Christians in quest of "eternal love."

Perhaps we ought to ask ourselves just what it is we seek—eternal life or eternal love. After all, what is eternal life without an eternal love? C. S. Lewis, referring to immortality, wrote, "For my own part I have never seen how a preoccupation with that subject at the onset could fail to corrupt the whole thing."[1] Yet many Christians today are pursuing immortality rather than relationship. The majority, no doubt, are consciously unaware of such an end. And yet for those who conclude that throughout this life God must remain an unfathomable enigma, immortality is the only viable pursuit.

Much like the devout Jews of old who sanctimoniously refused to speak or write God's holy name, Yahweh, these folk place an unspoken ban on discussions of His nature and being. This is done presumably to prevent intrusions on His sovereignty. The result of this policy is the bewildering spectacle of Christians who, in one breath, claim the irrelevance and impossibility of truly knowing God, while, in the next, express gratitude for an intimate, personal relationship with Him!

An intimate personal relationship, if we are to give the words their due definition, can only be experienced *like with like*. It is the height of absurdity to think intimate fellowship may be realized, for instance, between yourself and a water buffalo. Fundamental mutual reference points are essential.

> Then God said, 'Let us make a man—someone like ourselves, to be the master of all life upon the earth and in the skies and in the seas.' So God made man like his Master. Like God did God make man . . . .
>
> Genesis 1:26–27 (TLB)

When we read these remarkable lines in the first chapter of Genesis we are to understand that we can know something about God by looking at ourselves. All that this entails will be the subject of this chapter.

DOES GOD WANT US TO KNOW HIM?

Not only does God want us to know Him, but He places top priority on it.

> For I desired mercy, and not sacrifice; and the knowledge of God more than burnt offerings.
>
> Hosea 6:6

> Thus saith the Lord, Let not the wise man glory in his wisdom, neither let the mighty man glory in his might, let not the rich man glory in his riches: but let him that glorieth glory in this, that he understandeth and knoweth me, that I am the Lord . . . .
>
> Jeremiah 9:23–24

Just pause for a moment and ask yourself this question: Why wouldn't God want me to know Him?

Some assert that a revelation of the divine nature to man would increase the prospect of human pride. This eventuality is quite unlikely, however, since God will not reveal Himself to those who are not humble and pure of heart in the first place (Isa. 57:15). If He did, He would be contributing to their moral delinquency. God "resisteth the proud" and He has made it clear that it is the "pure in heart" who shall "see God."

THE IMPORTANCE OF UNDERSTANDING

There are those who regard knowledge as an evil to be avoided and understanding as wishful thinking. To them, the idea that man can involve himself with God in meaningful dialogue is ludicrous, and expounding knowledge as a virtuous pursuit is downright dangerous.

It is with utmost clarity that the Bible warns against the deceptive and futile nature of worldly wisdom. We are told unequivocally that "the wisdom of this world is foolishness with God . . ." (I Cor. 3:19). We cannot advocate a wisdom sustained only by the finite. This "wisdom" must be rejected as being wholly inadequate.

Yet this provides no basis whatsoever from which to categorically reject knowledge. The Bible tells us, "How blessed is the man who finds wisdom, and the man who gains understanding" (Prov. 3:13). The knowledge spoken of in the eighth chapter of I Corinthians as that which "makes arrogant" is not in itself evil. Paul in this passage is not discussing the merits of knowledge but rather the *manner* in which our knowledge is used. A. W. Tozer proclaims,

> We have never gone along with the tenderminded saints who fear to examine religious things lest God should be displeased. On the contrary, we believe that God's handiwork is so perfect that it invites inspection.[2]

There is a great need for us to understand first who God is, and second what He expects of us. There are multiplied hundreds of scriptures referring to understanding and knowledge. In fact, the word "understanding" or an equivalent is found some sixteen times in the first parable (the sower) when it is read synoptically.

In Proverbs, God speaks to us as a father would, in heart-to-heart fashion, revealing the source of understanding.

> Hear, ye children, the instruction of a father, and attend to know understanding . . . . Get wisdom, get understanding: forget it not; neither decline from the words of my mouth. Forsake her not, and she shall preserve thee: love her, and she shall keep thee. Wisdom is the principal thing; therefore get wisdom: and with all thy getting get understanding.
>
> Proverbs 4:1,5–7

> My son, if thou wilt receive my words, and hide my commandments with thee; so that thou incline thine ear unto wisdom, and apply thine heart to understanding; yea, if thou criest after knowledge, and liftest up thy voice for understanding; if thou seekest her as silver, and searchest for her as for hid treasures; then thou shalt understand the fear of the Lord, and find the knowledge of God. For the Lord giveth wisdom: out of his mouth cometh knowledge and understanding.
>
> Proverbs 2:1–6

The fear of the Lord is the beginning of wisdom:
and the knowledge of the Holy is understanding.
Proverbs 9:10

Why is it so crucial that we understand God and fully take to heart all that He has said here? Tozer shares some very interesting insights into the dangers of participating in cosmic guessing games.

> . . . the most portentous fact about any man is not what he at a given time may say or do, but what he in his deep heart conceives God to be like. We tend by a secret law of the soul to move toward our mental image of God. That our idea of God correspond as nearly as possible to the true being of God is of immense importance to us. Compared with our actual thoughts about Him, our creedal statements are of little consequence . . . A right conception of God is basic not only to systematic theology but to practical Christian living as well. It is to worship what the foundation is to the temple . . . Before the Christian church goes into eclipse anywhere there must first be a corrupting of her simple basic theology. She simply gets a wrong answer to the question, 'What is God like?' and goes on from there.[3]

NO DESIRE FOR UNDERSTANDING

There are quite a number of Christians who, despite the fact they do not know what God is like, and despite divine solicitations to seek and understand, have no desire whatsoever to address the matter.

Why is this? Well, for openers, knowledge is painful. It is far easier to rest in tradition, or in someone else's research, than it is to search for understanding as a "hidden treasure." In addition, once the value and nature of that treasure is perceived, it is painfully easy to spot imitations and synthetics regardless of how well they may be outlaid and embedded in sermons, hymns and Christian literature.

Speaking of hymns, it might be an interesting sidelight to discuss the theological implications of hymnals. They have, it seems, acquired a reverence these days roughly equivalent to the Bible. While the hymns may be inspirational, they are not inspired scripture.

Very few of us would declare a prepared statement without first scanning the text to ascertain its content. Yet how often will we, without hesitation, sing a declaration to God and man without reviewing the "script" first? This is the process whereby a substantial proportion of the Church is indoctrinated. Doctrine is thus acquired by osmosis rather than through Berean* quest.

Another reason knowledge is not pursued by many Christians is the fear that it will diminish faith. The warning of many reformers was that as knowledge and understanding increased, there would be a proportionate decrease in faith.

While the Bible is most certainly filled with admonitions to avoid the wisdom of the world (vain, humanistic philosophizing), it plainly encourages us to "add to (our) faith virtue; and to virtue, knowledge" (I Peter 1:5). We may also consider Gordon Olson's observation:

> If knowledge decreases faith, then God has no faith.

Others find it preferable to adhere to a nebulous, abstract understanding of God rather than discuss certain passages and questions that will, in their opinion, produce disunity.

This is truly a sad state of affairs. If the unity we are attempting to protect is rooted in love, then surely we are suffering from an unjustified fear of controversy. What can happen, so often in our effort to procure and maintain a sort of "lovey-dovey" Christian atmosphere, is that we forget that there are two ingredients in true unity—common unselfishness (love) and common understanding

*See Acts 17:10–11.

(knowledge). The result of this oversight is, as A. W. Tozer warns,

> Union for union's sake . . . unity is so devoutly to be desired that no price is too high to pay for it . . . truth is slain to provide a feast to celebrate the marriage of heaven and hell, and to support a concept of unity which has no basis in the word of God.[4]

Englishman Arnold Lunn shed some real light on the issue at hand when he said:

> The prevailing prejudice against controversy is partly due to our distrust of logical argument and partly to silly confusion which equates the quarrelsome with the controversial; silly because it is the *inability* to see another man's point of view which makes people quarrelsome, and the *ability* to understand the other man's position which makes a good controversialist.[5]

If the discussion is serious and if the ultimate objective is truth and not mere negation, then disagreement can contribute toward better understanding. Loren Cunningham (International Director of Youth With A Mission) once summed up the issue succinctly by suggesting that disagreements don't cause disunity, a lack of forgiveness does.

The Bible says "a fool does not delight in understanding. . . ." (Prov. 18:2). For many today, the emphasis on love and unity is nothing more than superficial buoyancy, a sort of fellowship "in the clouds." Heartily clasping and pumping hands beneath the cloud layer, their heads remain shrouded in theological "mist-icism". This is undoubtedly due to the fact that when we stop thinking about knowledge in the abstract, we have to admit that what interests us most is what involves us as persons. We have a modern-day "sin of ignorance" whereby people don't know and they don't want to know. This desire to be vague and abstract when it comes to our understanding of God reveals a deep lack of love and discipline.

In any earthly relationship in which the flame of love is burning with fervency, is there any lack of initiative in discovering every detail concerning the object of our love? The answer may be simply put: A lack of discipline on our part to seek fuller understanding of God's marvelous Person and character reveals the stark fact that we just don't care!

How shall we escape if we neglect so great a salvation? You must understand that God is not referring to passive ignorance but to the willing choice to remain ignorant.

> Thine habitation is in the midst of deceit; through deceit they *refuse to know me*, saith the Lord.
>
> Jeremiah 9:6

> Hear the word of the Lord, ye children of Israel: for the Lord hath a controversy with the inhabitants of the land, because there is no truth, nor mercy, nor knowledge of God in the land. . . . My people are destroyed for lack of knowledge: because thou hast *rejected knowledge,* I will also reject thee, that thou shalt be no priest to me: seeing thou hast forgotten the law of thy God, I will also forget thy children.
>
> Hosea 4:1,6

Theologian John Calvin in many of his writings refers to a God who cloaks Himself in mystery; a God who wills to hide far from inquisitive curiosity. Unfortunately this teaching has permeated many of the theological institutions of this country. How deeply it must grieve the heart of God to hear this teaching being propagated.

WHY DID GOD CREATE MAN?

Of all the questions that could be asked, this one is of vital importance. If we can answer this question, it will enable us to understand the very core of God's thinking concerning the type of relationship He desires with man.

Before proceeding, it is necessary that we first understand exactly what the Bible means when it says "God is love." There are four Greek words used to describe what our limited English vocabulary calls *love*. Of the four listed below, see if you are able to determine which definition properly belongs to God's character.

> Storge—A tender, motherly love—instinctual
> Eros—A physical or sexual love
> Phileo—A brotherly love—friendship, kindness
> Agape—An unselfish benevolence

If you chose *agape* you were right!

Why is this so important? Because it helps us understand God's *motivation* in creation. We are not merely interested in *what* God did but *why* He did it.

I have asked many Christians to give their opinion concerning God's motives and intentions in creating man. Most have given remarkably similar answers. "God created us to worship Him." "We were made to glorify God." "He created us for His pleasure."

Now let me ask *you* some further questions:

1) Is it not true that God is totally unselfish, willing our highest good without expecting anything in return? (*Agape* love)
2) Didn't God already have a host of beings praising and worshiping Him prior to man's creation?
3) Wouldn't God be egotistical in creating more beings for the express purpose of worshiping Him?

First, let me mention that the Bible does *not* say that God created men to worship Him. What it *does* say is that we were created for His pleasure. Now, in the light of the fact that God *is* love and that His love is a totally unselfish, giving love, why would God derive pleasure in creating man?

God has an enormous reservoir of love within His great being, and it needs an object of focus. A Being possessing a character of total, *agape* love derives great pleasure in creating further objects to serve as receptacles for His love. He wants to give and give of the great overflow of His love. Through sin and selfishness, we have lost all concept of this kind of love. We cannot conceive of a Being totally satisfied by giving without any internal strings attached to His love. But this is God. C. S. Lewis adds some intriguing thoughts about God's love:

> In that sense all His love is, as it were, bottomlessly selfless by very definition; it has everything to give and nothing to receive. . . . If the world exists not chiefly that we may love God but that God may love us, yet that very fact, on a deeper level, is so for our sakes. If He who in Himself can lack nothing chooses to need us, it is because we need to be needed . . . from nonentity to the beloved of God. . . .[6]

What a marvelous thought! The God of the universe speaks, and out of nothing the earth materializes in obedience to His word. Then this grand Being stoops to gather a handful of the freshly created substance. He uses it to form the shell of a man. Drawing in, He prepares to expel the most awesome, creative force in all the galaxies—the breath of God. Finally He falls in love with His man of dust—who moments earlier was a nonentity.

God designed man so that as he perceived and understood God's revelations of Himself it would be enjoyable to respond to this truth. This is praise; this is worship; this is glorifying God. *"Our highest activity must be response, not initiative."*[7] It is not worked up, it is a *natural* response to what we see. I believe David, like Adam and Eve, was loved by God because he *recognized* Him (Ps. 42:1–2). He admonishes in the Psalms to "sing praises with understanding," or, to put it in other words, sing "naturally."

We ought to see by now that God made man like Himself, not physically, but morally, in order to engage in a personal, intimate love relationship—like with like. If God is personal and has something in common with man, then there is *no* reason why He should not want to communicate truth about Himself in different ways to the minds of men.

If He really wanted to be mysterious and aloof, as Calvin taught, why did He give us His Word, perform miracles on earth, and send His Son? He would have been far more mysterious had He not expressed Himself in these ways. The overwhelming weight of evidence leads to the fact that God *wants* to communicate Himself.

> Or hath God assayed to go and take him a nation from the midst of another nation, by temptations, by signs, and by wonders, and by war, and by a mighty hand, and by a stretched out arm, and by great terrors, according to all that the Lord your God did for you in Egypt before your eyes? Unto thee it was showed, *that thou mightest know* that the Lord he is God; there is none else beside him.
>
> Deuteronomy 4:34–35

> Bow down thine ear, and hear the words of the wise, and apply thine heart unto *my knowledge*. For it is a pleasant thing if thou keep them within thee; they shall withal be fitted in thy lips. That thy trust may be in the Lord, I have *made known to thee* this day, even to thee. Have not I written to thee excellent things in counsels and knowledge, that I might *make thee know the certainty of the words of truth;* that thou mightest answer the words of truth to them that send unto thee?
>
> Proverbs 22:17–21

It is a wonderful passage, ". . . the *certainty* of the words of truth". Aren't you glad in this day and age that we can be certain about something?

Yet there are those "learned ones" who still insist that it's not in our best interest to try and get too close to God. It's almost sacrilegious to say that God can be understood and that you're attempting to understand Him. These individuals remind me of the disciples who tried to shoo away the little children when they attempted to get close to the Master. Jesus desired that we should understand the scriptures for He knew it was good for us to receive God's communication of Himself.

> Then opened he their understanding, that they
> might understand the Scriptures.
>
> Luke 24:45

God will in fact often go to great lengths to assist someone who is struggling to understand Him:

> And the angel of the Lord spake unto Philip, say-
> ing, Arise, and go toward the south, unto the way
> that goeth down from Jerusalem unto Gaza, which
> is desert. And he arose and went: and, behold, a
> man of Ethiopia, an eunuch of great authority
> under Candace queen of the Ethiopians, who had
> the charge of all her treasure, and had come to
> Jerusalem for to worship, was returning and sit-
> ting in his chariot reading Esaias the prophet.
> Then the Spirit said unto Philip, Go near, and join
> thyself to this chariot. And Philip ran thither to
> him, and heard him read the prophet Esaias, and
> said, *Understandest thou what thou readest?* And he
> said, How can I, except some man should guide
> me? And he desired Philip that he would come up
> and sit with him. . . . Then Philip opened his
> mouth, and began at the same Scripture, and
> preached unto him Jesus.
>
> Acts 8:26–31,35

Bible reading in many churches and homes has become
a pious routine, a religious symptom. The great desire of
the Ethiopian eunuch and the Jews of old to read God's
Word for *revelation*, to read it in order to understand God,
has waned. Let's go back in time, with the aid of
Nehemiah's descriptive narrative, to observe a most interesting and enlightening phenomenon—

> And all the people gathered as one man at the
> square which was in front of the Water Gate, and
> they asked Ezra the scribe to bring the book of the
> law of Moses which the Lord had given to Israel.
> Then Ezra the priest brought the law before the
> assembly of men, women, and all who could lis-
> ten with understanding . . . And he read from
> it . . . from early morning until midday, in the

presence of men and women, those who could understand; and all the people were attentive to the book of the law. . . . And Ezra opened the book in the sight of all the people for he was standing above all the people; and when he opened it, all the people stood up. Then Ezra blessed the Lord the great God. And all the people answered, 'Amen, Amen!' while lifting up their hands; then they bowed low and worshiped the Lord with their faces to the ground. . . . And the Levites, *explained the law* to the people while the people remained in their place. And they read from the book, from the law of God, translating *to give the sense so* that *they understood the reading.* Then Nehemiah . . . and Ezra the priest and scribe, and the Levites who taught the people said to all the people, 'This day is holy to the Lord your God; do not mourn or weep.' For all the people were weeping when they heard the words of the law. . . . So the Levites calmed all the people, saying, 'Be still, for the day is holy, do not be grieved.' And all the people went away to eat, to drink, to send portions and to celebrate a great festival, because they *understood* the words which had been made known to them.

Nehemiah 8:1–3,5–9,11–12 (NASB)

Let's sum up what we've observed:

1) The *people* asked to hear the Law.
2) It was read to those who could understand, as it was to be intellectually perceived.
3) It was read from early dawn to midday—that's at least six hours.
4) When the Word of God was opened, all the people stood up and then bowed and worshiped.
5) The Levites explained to the people what was being read so they would understand it.
6) All the people wept when they heard and understood the Law.
7) Finally they left to celebrate and rejoice because they understood the Word of the Lord.

To me, this is one of the most moving and remarkable scriptures I have ever read. It reveals the incredible result of realization. That we would return to reading and studying God's Word like these Jews! It's important that we remember the Bible *"is not a collection of embalmed truth,"* as A. W. Tozer astutely points out. Nor is it *"as some appear to think, God's last will and testament; it is, rather, the written expression of the mind of the living God."*[8]

God is fundamentally a creator, and He has not relegated Himself to using the printed word of the Holy Scriptures as the sole means to communicate Himself to man. The Bible itself only claims to be propositional truth about God and his dealings with man. Certainly all the vast realms of creation "declare" Him. His handiwork speaks distinctly of a master workman's presence. And there are many other sources of moral enlightenment, but none so eloquent or articulate regarding the nature of God's great heart and its expectations, as when He cloaked Himself with flesh and dwelt among us for thirty-three years. The man, Jesus, no less than the Son of God, came to earth to put the Godhead on exhibition. We read that

> (God) in these last days has spoken to us in His Son. . . . and He is the radiance of His glory and the exact representation of His nature. . . .
> Hebrews 1:2–3 (NASB)

> For God, who said, 'Light shall shine out of darkness,' is the One who has shone in our hearts to give the light (or revelation) of the knowledge of the glory of God in the face of Christ.
> 2 Corinthians 4:6 (NASB)

Jesus, who is referred to as the Word of God (Greek, *logos*), the mind of God in expression, stated clearly, "I have told you everything the Father told me."

THE DECEIVED AND THE DECEIVERS

Every individual in the world today can be classified as belonging to one of three groups of people: the deceived, the deceivers, or the reconciled. For the moment, we will concentrate on the first two groups. Who are the deceived and why are they deceived?

The deceived represent the majority of men who have never committed their lives to Jesus Christ, and who have no desire to respond to the moral enlightenment that they do have. In our American culture, this group is typified by the average Joe Six-pack sitting in front of the T.V. set with his feet propped up on the coffee table.

It is very important to keep in mind that *no man is deceived unless he wants to be deceived.*

> How long, O naive ones, will you love simplicity?
> And scoffers delight themselves in scoffing, and
> fools hate knowledge? . . . They hated knowledge,
> and did not choose the fear of the Lord.
>
> Proverbs 1:22,29 (NASB)

But what about those remote Pacific Islands, or the recluse tribes of South America, Africa or Indonesia? What about those who have never read the Bible—who have never heard of Jesus Christ?

There is a very interesting passage of scripture in the first chapter of Romans which answers this *very question* in great detail:

> For the wrath of God is revealed from heaven against all ungodliness and unrighteousness of men, who *suppress the truth* in (by) unrighteousness, because that which is known about God is evident within them. . . . For since the creation of the world His invisible attributes, His eternal power and divine nature, have been clearly seen, *being understood through what has been made, so that they are without excuse. For even though they knew God,* they did not honor Him as God, or give thanks; but they became futile in their speculations, and their foolish heart was darkened. . . . And just as *they did not see fit to acknowledge God any longer,* God gave them over to a depraved mind, to do those things which are not proper.
>
> Romans 1:18–21,28 (NASB)

To analyze what we have just read:

1) God is not angry with those who have little truth, but with those who *suppress* or hold down the truth by unrighteousness.
2) There are two major sources of moral enlightenment that all men have, regardless of where they live: a) their inner consciousness and b) nature.
3) These sources of revelation concerning God are not obscure, they are "clearly seen."
4) They "knew God" but did not honor Him as God and began to speculate or explain things away.
5) Thus, unrighteous men are left without excuse.

Romans 8:28 tells us that "they did not see fit to acknowledge God *any longer*." This seems to indicate that they had "known" God in some way previously. But how? We can go a long way toward answering this question by carefully examining the two universal sources of moral enlightment mentioned in this passage.

NATURE

> The heavens are telling the glory of God; and the firmament proclaims his handiwork. Day to day pours forth speech, and night to night *declares knowledge*. There is no speech, nor are there words; their voice is not heard; yet their voice goes out through all the earth, and their words to the end of the world.
>
> Psalm 19:1–4 (RSV)

When men are committed to living for themselves supremely, they cannot admit that the things God has made are wonderful, that they are testimonies to His wonderful character, and that they declare His glory. To do so would be tantamount to admitting disobedience and recognizing their responsibility to commit their lives to their Maker. This, then, is the basic intention behind the totally unfounded, foolish Theory of Evolution: *The message of God's creation must be silenced.* And "they became futile in their speculations . . ." (Romans 1:21).

CONSCIOUSNESS

> I have seen the task which God has given the sons of men with which to occupy themselves. He has made everything appropriate in its time. He has also set *eternity (Heb.: Olam) in their heart . . .*
>
> Ecclesiastes 3:10–11 (NASB)

The interesting thing here is that the Hebrew word "olam" carries the connotation of a *love of eternity* or *love of eternal things.* There is an inner longing inside every human being that will never be satisfied until he comes in contact with "the high and lofty One who inhabits eternity." It is this longing, "that of an unsatisfied desire which is more desirable than any other satisfaction," which C. S. Lewis called "joy." In his spiritual autobiography, he wrote:

> I had been equally wrong in supposing that I desired joy itself. Joy itself considered simply as an event in my own mind, turned out to be of no value at all. All the value lay in that of which joy was the desiring . . . Last of all I had asked if joy itself was what I wanted; and labeling it 'aesthetic experience,' had pretended I could answer Yes. But that answer too had broken down. Inexorably joy proclaimed, 'You want—I myself am your want of—something other, outside, not you nor any state of you.' I did not yet ask, who is the desired . . . But this brought me already into the region of awe . . .[9]

Who are the deceivers and why are they deceivers? The deceivers are a coalition of the religiously affiliated who know quite a lot about God but fail to relate to Him on a personal basis. They include faithful churchmen, Bible school and seminary graduates, fundamentalists and evangelicals. They are the people who are incredibly active doing good works under the banner of Jesus Christ, but who have never slowed down enough to get to know the One they think they are serving. Carnal theological professors, whose hearts may mutter in secret, "God has a wonderful plan for my life," have failed to realize that Christianity, in its naked essence, is nothing less than a relationship. Whatever else may issue forth from the Christian life must be rooted in that sublime relationship—God with the soul. Jesus incisively spoke to this group.

> Not everyone that saith unto me, Lord, Lord, shall enter into the kingdom of heaven; but he that doeth the will of my Father which is in heaven. Many will say to me in that day, Lord, Lord, have we not prophesied in thy name? and in thy name have cast out devils? and in thy name done many wonderful works? And then will I profess unto them, *I never knew you:* depart from me, ye that work iniquity.
>
> Matthew 7:21–23

What an eternally conclusive indictment! "I never knew you." What chilling words to come out of the mouth of God. So utterly unexpected. These people approached God on what they thought were familiar terms. They came using His name. As I read this passage over again, I noticed something I had never seen before, and it staggered me. One solitary word—"many". Jesus is not referring here to a small, isolated group. He says *many* will approach the Father on Judgment Day in this pathetic condition: spiritually barren and out of relationship.

I couldn't help asking: "But where do these people come from?" It is evident on two counts that they are not the clientele of local bars and brothels. First, they approached God with an air of familiarity. They assumed at least there would be some reciprocal recognition. Second, the works listed in this passage seem to indicate these individuals are ardently religious. Where, then, do they come from? The answer is, of course, from the churches.

These people are extremely harmful since they present a warped and incomplete rendering of the nature and character of God. Unfortunately, because of their words and deeds, it is easier for those in the world to rationalize their position.

There are, of course, those who do know God. Their lives are mobile portraits of God's character, although only miniature replicas of the one God painted on Calvary. This group has been reconciled to God. They have responded to God's mighty efforts to repair the relationship that was ruptured.

Each of these three groups have four basic concepts of God, and on the basis of these concepts their response to God is determined: *intimate, religious* or *blasphemous.*

	The Deceived	The Deceivers	The Reconciled
1	Unjust	Inscrutable	Reasonable
2	Tyrannical	Fixed	Creative
3	Vindictive	Legal	Loving
4	Alien	Mystical	Personal

BASIC ATTITUDES OF CHRISTIANS TOWARD THE LOST

I will give a further explanation of this diagram shortly, but first we need to deal with a basic attitude many believers have in regard to non-Christians. When expressed it often includes some combination of the following:

> "I don't have to explain God to anyone. It is their responsibility to simply believe Him at His Word. I can't save them! We can't understand God's ways anyway. We should stick to the simple gospel."

This is typical of the arrogant attitudes displayed by many Christians today. Though it may be cloaked in less offensive terminology, the underlying attitude is still present. Often, their unwillingness to answer specific questions and to thoroughly explain the plan and purpose of salvation is due to their own ignorance and lack of discipline. The "God said it—I believe it—that settles it" syndrome is sorely lacking that magical quality the Bible calls charity.

Our duty today is identical to that of John the Baptist— we are forerunners. "For you will go before the Lord to prepare His ways, to give to His people the knowledge of salvation" (Luke 1:76–77).

No, certainly we cannot save anyone ourselves. But we can inform people concerning their obligation to God and try to remove any misconceptions they may have so that when Jesus follows up they are ready for Him to salvage their lives. Peter admonishes us to always be "ready to make a defense to every one who asks you to give an account for the hope that is in you. . . ." (1 Peter 3:15).

The Bible is explicit in its teaching that an understanding of the Word of God is an imperative in salvation. Take the first parable, for example. In this parable both men *hear* the Word, yet one man is lost while the other bears fruit. What was the sole difference between them?

> Hear . . . the parable of the sower. When any one hears the word of the kingdom, and *does not understand it*, the evil one comes and *snatches away* what has been sown in his heart. . . . And the one on whom seed was sown on the good ground, this is the man who hears the word, and *understands it*; who indeed *bears fruit*. . . .
> Matthew 13:18–19,23 (NASB)

The so-called "simple gospel" is only simple if it is understood by our hearers. So often the plan of salvation has been oversimplified to the extent that it has been stripped of its health, vitality and very essence. It becomes instead an ugly, deformed collection of theological clichés. Only the man who hears *and* understands can be expected to produce any spiritual fruit.

Let's take a closer look at some of the basic concepts unbelievers have about God. These four misconceptions comprise the pillars of all the arguments that I have heard nonbelievers use to undergird their rejection of God.

1) God is *unjust!*
2) God is a *tyrant!*
3) God is *vindictive!*
4) God is *alien!*

How would you respond to questions that embody one or more of these false concepts about God? Did you ever wonder where people obtained these concepts?

I remember a conversation not long ago with a young humanist. This young man wasn't your run-of-the-mill, passive humanist. Educated at U.C.L.A., he devoted much time to propagating his ideas through journalistic channels including several campus newspapers. He picketed one of the largest churches in our area on several successive Sundays carrying a sign which read, "Let Man Live."

I don't think I'll ever forget my dumbfounded silence when, in response to my statement, "Jesus died for you," he replied almost sadly, "I wouldn't have wanted Him to." Response?

Maybe you've heard yourself lately, perhaps in response to current vogue, declaring, "I've been born again," only to be shocked by a sudden, "Great! What reincarnation are you in?" Response?

And then how do you deal with individuals who have *everything?* They are hard-working, happily-married, moral people who tell you life is great. Response?

Then there are those who have *nothing:* The Jew who rolls up his sleeve to reveal a tattoo that identifies him as a bearer of incomprehensible memories from his residency in a Nazi death camp. What do you do with him when he turns to you and says, "Never shall I forget that night . . . which has turned my life into one long night, seven times cursed and seven times sealed. Never shall I forget that smoke. Never shall I forget the little faces of the children, whose bodies I saw turned into wreaths of smoke beneath a silent, blue sky. Never shall I forget that nocturnal silence which deprived me, for all eternity, of the desire to live.

Never shall I forget those moments which murdered my God and my soul and turned my dreams into dust."[10] Response?

The responses and questions will be as diverse as people are, but the basic concepts of God are few. I hope you will try to *feel*, especially in this last case, part of the reason why it is so difficult for some to see God as just, and therefore, why they refuse to worship Him.

There are, I'm sad to say, throngs of cold-hearted Christians who, with a pedantic air, declare that God is *inscrutable*. This is a word that the Orientals have traditionally used to describe logic within the illogical. So these Christians, aghast at the insinuation that the facts do not speak of a good, just and loving God, declare that the facts are irrelevant and ought to be ignored.

Thrashing through their Bibles, they rush to find their pet scriptures which always work well in situations like these. Once armed with their scripture, they move abjectly away from the light of reality to their dark, obscure holes of theological abstraction.

> For my thoughts are not your thoughts, neither are your ways my ways, saith the Lord. For as the heavens are higher than the earth, so are my ways higher than your ways, and my thoughts than your thoughts.
>
> Isaiah 55:8–9

In their haste to wield their prized sword, they fail to notice they have gripped the weapon by the blade. Any scripture taken out of context becomes lethal to those who quote it, as well as to those who hear it. Isaiah 55:7 is rarely quoted along with verses 8 and 9 of the same chapter and the resultant concept is totally different than what God is attempting to convey.

> Let the wicked forsake his way, and the unrighteous man his thoughts: and let him return unto the Lord, and he will have mercy upon him: and to our God, for he will abundantly pardon.
>
> Isaiah 55:7

God is simply saying that His thoughts are *not like the unrighteous man's thoughts* and His *ways are not like those of the wicked*. The only difference here between God and man is in the elevation of his moral conduct. Once the unrighteousness and wickedness is repented of and forsaken, which is what God is pleading for in this scripture, then our ways and thoughts *are* like God's! When we are walking in obedience to God, then God doesn't think *differently*, only *better*.

Certainly no one enjoys tyrants, especially those employed by one. Whether it be a secretary, mail clerk, accountant or vice president, the result is predictable whenever requests are made or new ideas shared. Policy will remain unchanged; procedure will not be modified. Even before the entreaty or proposal reaches summation, the fist hits the desk and the *NO* is bellowed forth. The uncomfortable aspect of this situation lies in the knowledge that be there a tyrant, the *future* is as rigid as the present.

Here again we see the work of religious deceivers. They have eagerly disseminated the concept that God is *fixed*, and that *all* future events are seen as complete and consummated by Him. We've been told that God sees a person seeking truth in heaven or hell as a certainty. All this teaching is supposed to produce a warm sense of assurance in the hearts of believers everywhere. We have lovely plaques and decoupage hanging on our walls with the inscription, "Prayer Changes Things." Changes what? What can be changed if the future is fixed? Essentially, what you get when you adopt a God who is not able to think new thoughts, change His mind, realize changing circumstances and make new decisions, is a condition of static or motionlessness. It becomes a state of fate. It would be a pretty weak sovereign indeed who could not "handle" an influx of new data and crises without seeing them all first. This entire concept is not only unbiblical, but it fuels the world's concept of the rigid, stark, static tyrant of Judeo-Christianity.

Ever since the Garden of Eden, man has demonstrated belief in a vindictive God. The concept of vindictiveness is that of an eye for an eye, a tooth for a tooth. If you hurt me, I'm going to hurt you back. It is most interesting to note the behavior of Adam and Eve immediately subsequent to their sin. The fact that they hid themselves from One with whom they had enjoyed frequent intimate encounters is indicative of a radical change. Somehow, because *they* had changed, they thought *God* had changed. Down through history we have observed one pagan society after another engage in self-mutilation and self-torment as a kind of penance to appease the wrath of God. Even in our so-called civilized society, we have ample evidence that at least a residual belief in God's vindictiveness still exists.

One of the deceivers' most damaging deceptions centers around, of all events, the atonement. Like the Pharisees of old, they portray a God who is only interested in things *legal*. The idea perpetrated here probably is derived from the words "ransom" and "redeem" and in essence it is that Jesus *paid* in an exact, literal sense for our sins.[11] Although the Word of God repeatedly declares that Jesus Christ *bore* the sins of the world, they insist on presenting a vindictive God who demands a payment before He will forgive. Surely this is in obvious contradiction to Jesus' parable on forgiveness, where the man was forgiven his debt solely on the basis of compassion—without payment of any kind!

Certainly there were governmental considerations for God to weigh. There was the necessity to uphold the law and justify the Lawgiver in the issuance of a pardon in opposition to His words, "the soul that sinneth, it shall die." However, to in any way confuse God's *governmental role* with His *personal feelings* is a gross error. God has always wanted to forgive. He holds no grudges. Remember His agape love? He needed only to find a way to do it wisely. He is not bitter and does not want to be personally paid back for anything.

We will discuss the matter of redemption in a later chapter, but I trust you can see how the portrayal of a strictly legal God encourages many people to view Him as a vindictive Being. This was precisely what my humanist friend had in mind.

Then a large proportion of those who shrug God off do so because they view Him, if He exists at all, as distant and alien. It all goes back to the point we discussed earlier concerning the necessity of fellowship like with like if there is going to be intimacy. People simply cannot relate to a God they are convinced is irrelevant and divorced from their everyday lives.

This concept of God's impersonality has been fostered, to a great extent, by the inflamed, hyper-mysticism found in many churches today. This mysticism is due in part to the fact that often biblical descriptions of God's personal feelings are explained away by calling them *anthropopathisms*. An anthropopathism is when you attribute human feelings to God. We are told that God's emotions are described as being like ours only to help us to understand Him. My good friend Harry Conn asks, "If mad doesn't mean mad, or glad, glad or joyful, joyful—what do they mean?" To put it another way, when God is talking about His character using personal words that in essence are meaningless because they are nondescriptive of reality, the prospect of intimacy evaporates.

Fortunately there are no anthropopathic statements in the Bible. God feels and reacts exactly the way He says He does. Where God helps us semantically is in our understanding of His Being. For example, His power attributes are omnipresence and omnipotence. These semantic analogies are called *anthropomorphisms*. These statements we do indeed find in the scriptures. A good example would be "He shall cover thee with his feathers, and under his wings shalt thou trust. . ." (Psalm 91:4).

It has somehow become a symbol of spirituality to leave one's mind parked in the church foyer before entering the sanctuary. Many Christians, as we have said before, simply do not want to take the time and effort to get to know God. So alternately they will do a variety of things to produce "spiritual goose bumps" in the realm of the mystical.

It is true that Christianity is a relationship to be *experienced*. But since our emotions respond to what our minds think, Christianity is experienced both *intellectually* and *emotionally*. The latter flows from the former. Again this is what David meant when he encouraged us to "sing praises with understanding."

WHAT WE MUST KNOW ABOUT GOD

There have been books written in recent days stating that the only vital ingredient in salvation is faith. The important thing is not that we understand but that *we believe!* I'm indebted to Mr. Conn for the use of one more illustration: Suppose I were standing before your church group as a visiting guest speaker from Korea. I had an interpreter with me, but I neglected to use him at all during the course of my thirty-minute message. Then, putting my hand on my interpreter's shoulder, I say to him, "Now ask them if they believe what I've just said." What do you think the response of the English-speaking audience would be? "How can we believe what he's said—we don't even understand it!"

This is exactly the point Jesus made in His parable of the sower. We need to understand something before we can give—or *should* give our lives to God. A man doesn't need to know a *lot* in order to come to Christ, but he does need to understand something, and then live up to that something.

There are those who resist embracing any theology at all. They are put off by doctrines or any attempt to explain God. To "feel God" or "sense His presence" is for them the only matter of consequence. "Experiencing God" is certainly in current vogue and the thrust of a growing number of churches. What has happened experientially to many of these "anti-doctrine" people may have been real, and was certainly exciting;

> . . . but nothing comes of it. It leads nowhere—
> there is nothing to do about it. In fact, that is just
> why a vague religion—all about feeling
> God . . . and so on—is so attractive. It is all thrills
> and no work . . . but you will not get eternal life
> by simply feeling the presence of God . . .[12]

In other words, if we are going to know God, grow in grace, and shed old character traits, we must do more than feel. We must *obey*. To obey, we must know and trust our

Commander. We must understand His orders—not the *why* necessarily, but the *what*, and that means we must give attention to doctrine.

> Be diligent to present yourself approved to God as a workman who does not need to be ashamed, handling accurately the word of truth.
>
> 2 Timothy 2:15 (NASB)

> All Scripture is given by inspiration of God, and is profitable for doctrine . . . for instruction . . .
>
> 2 Timothy 3:16

Now, when we look at God there are two fundamental things we can say about Him: He is *uncreated* and He is a *creator*. If you will look closely at these two words, you will notice that one is a *fact* while the other represents a *choice*. All God's attributes can be summed up under one or the other of these fundamental aspects.

GOD

Uncreated	*Creator*
(Metaphysical—or what He is)	(Moral—or what He chooses to do with what He is)
His Being	His Character
Power Attributes	*Moral Attributes*
Omnipotence	Holiness
Omniscience	Love
Omnipresence	Justice
Etc.	Etc.
This is not necessarily a vital part of our understanding.	This we *must* know!

How many who are married felt that it was imperative to thoroughly understand the physical abilities of their partner before committing their life to them? How many of you ladies took your prospective husband down to a track and timed his exertion in the 100-yard dash, or drove him to a gym in order to obtain a tape measurement of his biceps? Sound ridiculous? Of course it is. I'm quite sure, on the other hand, that most of you would agree it is absolutely vital to know a person's *character* before committing your entire earthly life to them.

Doesn't it make sense to admonish the non-Christian to understand God's character before committing themselves to an *eternal* relationship? When the world asks us questions that relate to God's character, and we respond by saying that we can't understand God's ways, we are dangerously distorting the picture. No, I cannot understand God's omnipotence, nor can I explain how He can be present everywhere simultaneously. But I don't commit myself to God because He is omnipresent or omnipotent. I commit myself to Him because He is loving, just and kind!

We must distinguish between God's Being, what He *is*, and His character or what He has *chosen* to do with what He is. Only when this is understood will we cease our foolish and dangerous generalizations that we cannot understand God.

The God concepts of the reconciled reflect a *true* understanding of His character. We can tell the man who thinks God is unjust that He is not arbitrary but *reasonable* in all His dealings with men. God will share His reasons with any sincere seeker to whom the information is necessary to bring that person to Himself.

To the man who views God as a tyrant, we can reveal a Being of unceasing *creativity*, a God of flexibility who is never arbitrary and whose hands are not tied by fate. For those who secretly fear a vindictive supreme being, there is a great need to understand the unconditional *love* of God. Finally, to those who through Calvinistic theology, or some other means, have come to consider God as an alien, we must introduce a *personal* God who cries out for them to know Him intimately. Much theology presents God in such a light that He resembles some type of Eastern philosophical greatness. This I'm sure must bring unspeakable grief to a God who longs to be recognized as a living and loving personality. If we made known a God who was reasonable, creative, loving, and personal, it wouldn't be easy for the world to resist Him.

Therefore, since we have this vital ministry let us not be:

> . . . walking in craftiness or adulterating the word of God, but by commending ourselves to every man's conscience in the sight of God. And even if our gospel is veiled (covered), it is veiled to those who are perishing.
>
> 2 Corinthians 4:2-3 (NASB)

WHAT IS SALVATION?

Jesus undoubtedly summed it up best at the beginning of His high priestly prayer when He said, "And this is life eternal, that they might *know* thee the only true God, and Jesus Christ, whom thou hast sent" (John 17:3). In I Timothy we find the words—"to be saved and to come to the *knowledge of the truth*" (I Tim. 2:4).

We need to exercise caution that we not become religiously obese, constantly taking in spiritual knowledge and never making a heart commitment to the truth—one who is "always learning and never able to come to the knowledge (or recognition) of the truth" (2 Tim. 3:7).

> Making mention of you in my prayers; that the God of our Lord Jesus Christ, the Father of glory, may give to you a spirit of wisdom and of revelation in the knowledge of him. I pray that the eyes of your heart may be enlightened, so that you may know what is the hope of His calling, ... walk in a manner worthy of the calling with which you have been called.
>
> Ephesians 1:16-18; 4:1 (NASB)

HOLINESS

2/LIVE WHAT YOU KNOW

Purity of hearts is not maturity of Christian experience.

Duncan Campbell

If a moral agent can know what end he aims at or lives for, he can know, and cannot but know, at all times, whether he is right or wrong. All that upon this theory a moral agent needs to be certain of is, whether he lives for the right end.

Charles G. Finney

Therefore to him that knoweth to do good, and doeth it not, to *him* it is sin.

James 4:17

In any love relationship, one of the primary goals is to discover the expectations of the loved one and, to the best of our ability, fulfill them. We discussed in the last chapter the tremendous importance of knowing God and what He expects of us. It is what God expects of us that will be the subject of this chapter.

WHAT DOES GOD EXPECT OF US?

God makes His standards and expectations quite clear in His Word. So clear, in fact, that many theologians have attempted to cloud these passages to prevent the intensity of God's revelation from bothering the average parishioner.

But as he which hath called you is holy, so *be ye holy* in all manner of conversation; because it is written, Be ye holy; for I am holy.

1 Peter 1:15–16

34

> Now when Abram was ninety-nine years old, the
> Lord appeared to Abram and said to him, 'I am
> God Almighty; walk before Me, and *be blameless.'*
>
> Genesis 17:1 (NASB)

> Having therefore these promises, dearly beloved,
> let us *cleanse ourselves* from all filthiness of the
> flesh and spirit, *perfecting holiness* in the fear of
> God.
>
> 2 Corinthians 7:1

> *Be ye therefore perfect*, even as your Father which is
> in heaven is perfect.
>
> Matthew 5:48

There you have it. God's standard is *holiness* and *perfection*. Do you resent it? Do you feel the urge to argue the point? Many do. But to tone down God's expectations constitutes tampering with the words of the Almighty, an incredibly foolish and dangerous activity for anyone to be involved in.

There are many today whose lives do not correspond to the biblical standard of holiness. When one finds himself in this situation he has two options available:

1) Lower the biblical standard to correspond to his present conduct.
2) Elevate his conduct to correspond to the biblical standard.

Unfortunately, the first option often becomes the designated solution. In the process of denying personal holiness as an attainable state, the very essence of what God desires in relationship with man is shunned. The fact that so many are denying the possibility of leading a truly holy life reveals either a mass desire to justify their love of pleasure more than God, or a profound ignorance as to the nature and definition of biblical holiness.

WHAT IS HOLINESS?

When we ask ourselves this question, we need to look at the very nature of God Himself, for it was He who said, "Be ye holy; for *I am holy*" (1 Peter 1:16). God is referred to as being *light* (I John 1:5) and *love* (I John 4:8). A brief description of these elements of God's character will enable us to grasp more fully the implications of holiness.

LOVE

"Agape love" is a term which may be defined as a "disinterested (not to be confused with uninterested) benevolence." In other words, an unselfish willing for the highest good.

LIGHT

The term "light" is an expression referring to that which reveals to us what our actions ought to be. The Bible states "whatsoever doth make manifest is light." Light is also used in the Bible to connote understanding or perception.

Holiness can therefore be defined as living for the highest good of God and our fellow man according to our knowledge of what that entails at any given time. Or, to put it another way, it is simply living up to the light you have from a right intention of heart.

WHY LIVE FOR GOD'S HIGHEST GOOD?

There are some people who consider it downright selfish of God to require the creatures He made to choose Him supremely and to focus their attention on *who He is* and *what He is doing*. This, however, is far from being the case. The Bible says that "God is light, and in him is no darkness at all" (1 John 1:5). What this means is that God's moral character is absolutely perfect, that He is presently living up to all that His intelligence tells Him He should be doing. This is why He can be called a holy Being. God is not holy because He is holy. He is holy because He chooses to use all His attributes in a loving (*agape*) way. Holiness involves choice and enlightenment.

We choose the things we do in life on the basis of their value. We would not, for example, find many housewives shopping for cooking utensils in the children's toy department, even if the price tags on little girls' cooking sets matched those in the housewares section. Again, if a wealthy friend took you to the nearest sewing machine retailer with an insistent offer to foot the bill on whatever machine you liked, the chances are that you would not browse around the $50 used models. Now, in these cases, it is the value factor that obligates a choice of merchandise in keeping with the light or understanding you have on the matter.

As God lovingly and wisely surveys His created universe, He is acutely aware that in order to will *our* highest good He must will His *own* highest good. The happiness of all creation hangs dependent upon His well-being. God recognizes the intrinsic value of His own being as the ultimate value in the entire universe. As a result, He unselfishly requires us to choose Him supremely for our own well-being. If, as God surveyed the universe, He was able to discover something more valuable than Himself, He would, acting in wisdom, require us to choose that end instead.

When an object is perceived or understood by the mind to be intrinsically valuable (valuable in and of itself), we cannot help but choose or refuse it. In other words, if we choose any object other than that which we have come to understand as possessing intrinsic value, we are making a deficient choice. A *knowingly* deficient choice the Bible calls *sin*.

OUR ULTIMATE INTENTION
IS WHAT COUNTS

I don't suppose anyone knows, even with the aid of modern computers, the number of choices made during the course of an average lifetime. The answer, if it were ever published, would probably stagger our imagination.

All of the choices we make in our lives can be classified into three categories according to their relative importance. Once they are categorized, we begin to notice that in spite of the astronomical number of choices we make, life is actually pretty simple!

SUPREME CHOICE

May only be made for the highest good of God and your fellow man
or
for the gratification of self.

SUBORDINATE CHOICES

The means and choices to secure our ultimate choice.

SIMPLE CHOICES

The actual carrying out of our subordinate choices, which are essentially a furthering of our supreme choice.

Question: Which level of choice do you think God looks at to determine what is virtuous and what is sinful?

Before we answer our own question, let's examine a brief scriptural commentary on the subject.

> Woe to you, scribes and Pharisees, hypocrites! For you clean the outside of the cup and of the dish, but inside they are full of robbery and self-indulgence. You blind Pharisee, first clean the inside of the cup and of the dish, so that the outside of it may become clean also. Woe to you scribes and Pharisees, hypocrites! For you are like whitewashed tombs which on the outside appear beautiful, but inside they are full of dead men's

bones and all uncleanness. Even so you too out-
wardly appear righteous to men, but inwardly you
are full of hypocrisy and lawlessness.

Matthew 23:25–28 (NASB)

Therefore do not go on passing judgment before
the time, but wait until the Lord comes who will
both bring to light the things hidden in the darkness and disclose the motives of men's hearts; and
then each man's praise will come to him from
God.

1 Corinthians 4:5 (NASB)

And He said to them, "Are you too so uncom-
prehending? Do you not see that whatever goes
into the man from outside cannot defile him; because it does not go into his heart, but into his
stomach, and is eliminated?' . . . . And He was
saying, 'That which proceeds out of the man, that
is what defiles the man. For from within, out of
the heart of men, proceed the evil thoughts and
fornications, thefts, murders, adulteries. . . . All
these evil things proceed from within and defile
the man."

Mark 7:18–21,23 (NASB)

Keep thy heart with all diligence; for out of it are
the issues of life.

Proverbs 4:23

These are just a few of the many scriptures in the Bible
which make it abundantly clear that it is our ultimate intention or supreme choice in life that is the source of all our
choices—major and minor, good or evil.

Robert Ringer in his smash best seller *Looking out for #1*
(over one year on the *N.Y. Times* best seller list) describes
this process in the pursuit of self-gratification.

When you boil it all down . . . everyone's main
objective in life is—to feel good . . . we sometimes lose sight of the fact that our primary objective is really to be as happy as possible and that

all our other objectives, great and small, are only a means to that end.[1]

To further emphasize the point, let's look at the lives of two young men going into the ministry.

YOUNG MAN #1		YOUNG MAN #2
To live for God	*SUPREME CHOICE*	To live for self supremely
Trains in college and seminary to become minister/ evangelist.	*SUBORDINATE CHOICES*	Trains in college and seminary to become minister/ evangelist.
Purchases new Bible and books and drives to school.	*SIMPLE CHOICES*	Purchases new Bible and books and drives to school.

God tells us that man has a tendency to look on the outward appearance (1 Sam. 16:7). That being the case, what would most people determine about the life of the second man in our diagram? No doubt that he was a dedicated Christian with a genuine desire to serve God. However, if the truth of the matter were known, God considered this young man's training to be an abomination in His sight. The reason? This young man loved to please himself more than anything else in the world. He craved attention and felt it could be secured through an evangelistic platform ministry. He spent time imagining all those faces looking at him and waiting for him to stretch forth his hand of power in their direction. This was intensely gratifying to his ego. Yet some preparation for this great task was needed, so he attended seminary. No matter though, all that knowledge he would obtain in seminary would just be all the more prestigious.

So although the actions and choices of these two young men were nearly identical, one of them produced evil, corrupt fruit while the other, whose ultimate intention of heart was to live for God supremely, produced good fruit.

The Bible teaches us that unless our ultimate or supreme choice is right, no deed or decision at a lower level is worthy of anything on Judgment Day.

> A good tree cannot bring forth evil fruit, neither can a corrupt tree bring forth good fruit. Every tree that bringeth not forth good fruit is hewn down, and cast into the fire.
>
> Matthew 7:18–19

When we use the terms supreme choice or ultimate intention we use them as synonyms for "heart," or purpose in life. When we ask Jesus into our hearts, it is important that we make no mistake about the fact that we are asking him to take over our purpose in life.

Holiness and moral character can *only* be determined by observing the *intention*. *Actions* will rarely give us a true picture.

What is most confusing and distressing to many Christians is that, while they discern their intentions and motives to be right, they often make errors in conduct. The notion that holiness is a state which can never literally be realized proceeds from the erroneous linkage of holiness with *conduct* rather than *motive*. This is why most Christians will cling to the idea that holiness is something only obtained in heaven. Others adhere to an abstract idea of living in Christ's holiness, even though their lifestyle does not reflect it.

Holiness isn't something you can borrow—you either have it or you don't. The theological doctrine of "imputed righteousness" has been grossly distorted in our day. We are told that God looks at us through the blood of Christ and sees us as righteous, regardless of our actual state.

Let's stop kidding ourselves. God sees us exactly the way we *are*. If we are living in obedience, He sees it. If we are living selfish, unholy lives, we can be sure He sees that too.

> The Lord has rewarded me according to my righteousness; according to the cleanness of my hands He has recompensed me. For I have kept the ways of the Lord, and have not wickedly departed from my God. . . . I was also blameless with Him, and I kept myself from my iniquity. Therefore, the Lord has recompensed me according to my righteousness; according to the cleanness of my hands in His eyes.
>
> Psalm 18:20–21,23–24 (NASB)

Now, whose righteousness is David talking about here—Christ's? No! *David* has "kept the ways of the Lord," and God is obviously pleased with him. Please don't misunderstand what I'm saying. The Bible does indeed teach that Christ's righteousness is imputed to us. This righteousness, however, cannot be imputed as a *technicality*. It can only come to us through *relationship*. In other words, as I spend time with God, watching Him, listening to Him and emulating Him, I will begin to take on His characteristics and likeness. Do you know how David came to the place where he was able to speak about his righteousness as he did? Here's a little secret from his memoirs:

> My soul longeth, yea, even fainteth for the courts of the Lord: my heart and my flesh crieth out for the living God.
>
> Psalm 84:2

> O God, thou art my God; early will I seek thee: my soul thirsteth for thee, my flesh longeth for thee . . . . my soul followeth hard after thee . . . .
>
> Psalm 63:1,8

> As the hart panteth after the water brooks, so panteth my soul after thee, O God.
>
> Psalm 42:1

The righteousness of Christ is imputed to us as a *reality*—something that is literally manifest in our lives. It only comes, however, through the interaction of a relationship. There is no "technical" righteousness. There is no righteousness apart from relationship. The righteousness of Christ is never imputed unless it is imparted.

> A pupil is not above his teacher; but everyone, after he has been fully trained, will be like his teacher.
>
> Luke 6:40 (NASB)

MOTIVE AND CONDUCT

While we are discussing the matter of conduct, it is important that we consider the fact that *right action can only follow right understanding*. If our ultimate intention is set to love God supremely (keeping in mind the full implications of the word love), then this is essentially all that we need to think about. We do not need to be under constant pressure to monitor our conduct each moment of the day. If you are making certain subordinate choices or everyday simple choices which to the best of your knowledge are the right means to fulfill your ultimate choice in life, and you are *mistaken*, this is *by no means sin*. The Bible states, "Therefore to him that *knoweth to do good*, and doeth it not, *to him* it is sin" (James 4:17). God is saying that we are responsible for what we know—nothing more and nothing less.

> The secret things belong unto the Lord our God; but those things which are revealed belong unto us and to our children forever, that we may do all the words of this law.
>
> Deuteronomy 29:29

Our judicial system takes this principle into consideration when defendants are charged with a crime. If an individual has ignorantly or mistakenly conducted himself in the wrong manner, he oftimes will be exonerated in a court of law. This procedure, however, cannot be repeated, for coupled to the forgiveness is an *increase in knowledge* as to the proper course of action in the future. Jesus, although He forgave the adulterous woman, commanded her to go her way and "sin no more."

Little children also assume that their *motives* are the important consideration when they are accused of some type of wrongdoing. Many times a desperate little cry of "I didn't mean to!" is a most effective deterrent to punishment.

For those accused of premeditated crime, however, there must be no recourse. For while it is safe to pardon one who erred unintentionally, it is a menace to society when one guilty of *intentional harm* is released. The motives and intentions are the determining factor.

How often our own hearts have been touched by the unsophisticated, flimsy gifts of children on special occasions. When a guest chuckles at the gift, we reply with a touch of indignation, "It's the thought (intention) that counts"! We don't feel slighted by the fact that gift wasn't expensive. There was no obligation for the child to give more because it was beyond his means. It is conversely true that when someone *does* have the means of elegant expression and a lackluster gift is given, it is the thought that counts, this time in a negative sense.

To further illustrate the relationship of motive and conduct, I'll let you in on one of the less clever moments in my life:

> On the far end of the counter in our kitchen there was a glass container normally filled with small, plastic packets of vitamins. Often after an evening meal or snack I transferred a pack of vitamins from the jar to my body where I assumed they did more good.
>
> Later one evening after completing this healthy ritual, I began to experience a burning sensation in my arms and legs that slowly crept over my entire body. Although at first I didn't give it much thought, the sensation increased so markedly that I went into the bathroom and looked in the mirror. After looking at my face, which had become blood red, I became perceptibly alarmed.

> Moving downstairs I revealed the condition to my mother who asked if I had taken any medication recently. After commenting that I didn't remember taking anything other than vitamins from the kitchen jar, she began to laugh. I didn't know whether to feel insulted or encouraged! Finally she was able to explain what was so humorous. As it turned out I had taken my sister's weight-reduction pills designed to flush out the capillaries. Some people react quite strongly and, as I had no need or intention to lose weight, I turned out to be one of those people.

Gordon Olson, a man who many consider to be one of the great theologians of our day, often gives the account of his young grandson, who, in a spontaneous act of affection, crawled up into his lap and accidentally knocked the glasses off his face. Unfortunately, they wound up on the floor in pieces.

Now, the common denominator in both of these cases is that *the intention or motive was right, while the conduct was deficient due to a lack of knowledge or understanding.*

WE CANNOT SERVE TWO MASTERS

One more point about this matter of our supreme choice. You may have noticed that while subordinate choices and simple choices are *plural,* the supreme choice is *singular.* This is due to the fact that on this level of intention only *one* choice exists. You can choose to live for yourself supremely or God supremely, but *you cannot live for both simultaneously.*

> No man can serve two masters. . . .
>
> > Matthew 6:24

> He that is not with me is against me. . . .
>
> > Matthew 12:30

> Doth a fountain send forth at the same place sweet water and bitter? Can the fig tree, my

brethren, bear olive berries? either a vine, figs? so can no fountain both yield salt water and fresh.

James 3:11—12

Their heart is divided; now shall they be found faulty: he shall break down their altars, he shall spoil their images.

Hosea 10:2

When a man tries to live for God and for himself at the same time, he soon discovers it is impossible, and unless he repents his life will end up a torn wreck. This is what the Bible warns against when it says "a double-minded man is unstable in all his ways" (James 1:8).

Motive & Conduct Combinations	Is it Possible?	Explanation
Right motive— Right conduct	Yes	This is an example of a life of holiness.
Right motive— Wrong conduct	Yes	This life is also holy if the error in conduct was made due to lack of knowledge.
Wrong motive— Wrong conduct	Yes	This is an example of a life of selfishness.
Wrong motive— Right conduct	No	This is also a life of selfishness. Although conduct may appear good, it isn't virtuous.
Right motive— Wrong motive	No	This is impossible. No man can serve two masters.

WILL ONE SIN SEND ME TO HELL?

There is ample scripture to assure anyone attempting to live a life apart from God that one violation of God's moral law is all that is necessary to make them a rebel in God's moral government and deserving of death. The question on most people's mind is "But what about the Christian who sins"?

When individuals commit their entire lives to Jesus Christ in salvation, a fundamental change occurs in their relationship to God. Where before we were only *subjects in God's moral government* now we have become *children in His household.* God becomes our heavenly Father and "whom (a father) loveth he chasteneth" (Prov. 3:12,16 and Heb. 12:6). No, one sin will not get us booted out of God's household, but it will get us a spanking. If we persist, however, in doing those things that are displeasing to God, then the basic love relationship is put in a precarious position.

Most children fortunate enough to have been brought up in a home where the parents were in love have, nonetheless, likely seen their parents in an occasional spat. Even though these times were unpleasant, it would be ridiculous to look upon an isolated incident and conclude that the parents were no longer in love. If, on the other hand, their conduct was such that they were consistently and knowingly hurting each other, the child would begin to question whether or not there was indeed a *motive of love.*

To sum up what we have said on the subject of holiness, let's keep in mind that:

1) God expects us to be holy or perfect.
2) This holiness is a perfection of motive or heart intention.
3) We cannot simultaneously lead a holy life and a selfish life.
4) Holiness is living up to all the light we have at any given time.
5) The seriousness of sin is weighed according to our understanding of what the will of God is.

When the Bible talks about sin as a *manner of life,* it always refers to it in the *past tense.* We must necessarily, and in an act of repentance, turn away from *all known sin* and humbly reach out to Jesus to cleanse us from our sin and forgive our unrighteousness. If we have not done this, then we have never experienced salvation.

You do not need to know a great deal in order to be a Christian or to be holy, but you must be willing to respond by living up to what you do know. It is just as possible for a two-week-old Christian to live a holy life as it is for a seasoned, mature Christian. We quoted Duncan Campbell at the start of the chapter, "Purity of heart is not (necessarily) maturity of Christian experience." The mature Christian has a great deal more understanding to be sure, but he is therefore responsible to live up to a great deal more than the babe in Christ. Moral character is what we are doing with our capability of moral response and the amount of light we possess.

SIN

3/A RACE OF REBELS

Every one who practices sin also practices lawlessness; and sin is lawlessness.

I John 3:4 (NASB)

The wrongness of the sinful act lies not merely in its nonconformity, or its departure from the accepted, appropriate way of behavior, but in an implicitly aggressive quality—a ruthlessness, a hurting, a breaking away from God and from the rest of humanity . . . alienation or (an) act of rebellion.

Dr. Karl Menninger

The Earth is also polluted by its inhabitants, for they transgressed laws, violated statutes (and) broke the everlasting covenant.

Isaiah 24:5 (NASB)

In his definition of the nature of sin, Dr. Menninger goes on to say:

Sin has a willful, defiant, or disloyal quality; someone is defied or offended or hurt. The willful disregard or sacrifice of the welfare of others for the welfare or satisfaction of the self is an essential quality of the concept of sin.[1]

That's a fine definition, even coming from a man who makes no profession of faith in Jesus Christ. Even Webster's Dictionary gives a better definition of sin than do most "born again" Christians:

Sin is transgression of the law of God; disobedience of the divine will, moral failure. Sin is failure

> to realize in conduct and character the moral ideal, at least as fully as possible under existing circumstances; failure to do as one ought toward one's fellowman.

Sin has lost its prominence and most certainly its popularity as a sermon theme for clergymen searching for a word to pass onto their congregations. It isn't so much that preaching on sin and guilt has lost its effectiveness as it is a matter of contemporary pastoral preference. In the foreboding and depressing atmosphere of our troubled times, a man of the cloth, if he is to enjoy success, must give attention to inspirational themes. Topics revolving around love, unity and grace are "hot" sermons and very much in demand by religious constituencies; while messages having to do with sin, guilt and repentance are currently experiencing a steady decline. The popularity of the new "freedom messages" is indicative of the direction of the church. "Inner Healing," a la Ruth Carter Stapleton, and the PMA (positive mental attitude) seminars are prime examples of the trend away from piercing sermons on guilt and sin.

We have witnessed the arrival of the day when the church has begun to place more emphasis on the *results* of sin than on sin itself. We have observed the shocking metamorphosis of sin as it discards its old cocoon of personal, moral responsibility to take on the form of a *sickness*. It seemed strange to begin this chapter with a definition of sin. Yet today it seems there are more views on sin than there are flavors of ice cream. People embrace doctrines like they do almost everything else in our society, donning whatever is in fashion, and thus the need for definition. It is reminiscent of the day on Mount Sinai when God, as a result of the lost relationship, had to *write down* man's moral obligations.

About a decade ago prominent psychiatrist Dr. Karl Menninger lectured a group of young seminarians at Princeton Theological Seminary. It was here that he first began to sense, as he put it, the "anxious and unsettled feelings" within the clergy. After several more years of evaluating the problem, he stated "they have become shaken reeds, smoking lamps, earthen vessels . . . spent arrows. They have lost heart." The intoxication of success combined with the fear of failure has affected far too many ministers of the gospel. The net result is a series of sermons tailored (often subconsciously) to suit the people.

> And they come unto thee as the people cometh, and they sit before thee as my people, and they hear thy words, but they will not do them: for with their mouth they show much love, but their heart goeth after their covetousness.
>
> Ezekiel 33:31

> My sheep wandered through all the mountains, and upon every high hill: yea, my flock was scattered upon all the face of the earth, and none did search or seek after them. Therefore ye shepherds; hear the word of the Lord; . . . . Thus saith the Lord God; Behold, I am against the shepherds; and I will require my flock at their hand, and cause them to cease from feeding the flock; neither shall the shepherds feed themselves any more; for I will deliver my flock from their mouth, that they may not be meat for them.
>
> Ezekiel 34:6–7,10

SOME ERRONEOUS CONCEPTS OF SIN

Famous attorney Clarence Darrow delivered the following address to the prisoners in the Cook County Jail:

> There is no such thing as a crime as the word is generally understood. I do not believe there is any sort of distinction between the real moral conditions of the people in and out of jail. One is just as good as the other. The people here can no more help being here than the people outside can avoid being outside. I do not believe people are in jail because they deserve to be. They are in jail simply because they cannot avoid it on account of circumstances which are entirely beyond their con-

trol and for which they are in no way responsible . . . There are a great many people here who
have done some of these things (murder, theft,
etc.) who really do not know themselves why they
did them. It looked to you at the time as if you
had a chance to do them or not, as you saw fit;
but still, after all you had no choice . . . If you
look at the questions deeply enough and carefully
enough you will see that there were circumstances
that drove you to do exactly the thing which you
did. You could not help it. . . .[2]

This address is supportive of the doctrine of *causation,
determinism* or *inevitability.* During our investigation into the
five major theological-philosophical errors concerning the
nature of sin, notice how this concept of causation and inevitability plays a prominent role.

SIN IS A SICKNESS
False Concept 1

This is precisely what we are currently hearing from
all quarters. Psychologists, criminologists, lawyers, and
sociologists are singing in unison for the rehabilitation of
the unfortunate, sick element in our society. Punishment is
out of the question because it is applicable only when an individual is responsible for what he does. We are living in an
age when criminals possess more rights than victims; an era
when a tolerant lawyer will enlist the expertise of a
humanitarian psychologist to prove to an unbiased and just
court that to prosecute constitutes cruel and unusual treatment.

Once again, Dr. Menninger asks:

Is no one any longer guilty of anything? Is it only
that someone may be stupid or sick . . . ? Is no
one responsible, no one answerable for these acts?
Anxiety and depression we all acknowledge, and
even vague guilt feelings; but has no one committed any sin?[3]

The thing we ought to find most frightening of all, however, is the fact that more and more Christians are jumping on this bandwagon. One prominent Christian author refers to the "*sin infection,*" contending that when Adam sinned "that one sin *infected* the whole human race, still in his loins, with the *sickness* of sin and death. Since then, all men are born sinners with the sentence of death upon them. It's a fatal *disease* with only one known cure."[4] The implications of this mentality are given in verse in Anna Russel's "Psychiatric Folksong."

> At three I had a feeling of
>   Ambivalence toward my brothers,
> And so it follows naturally
>   I poisoned all my lovers.
> But now I'm happy; I have learned
>   The lesson this has taught;
> That everything I do that's wrong
>   Is someone else's fault.[5]

In a world of lenience, tolerance and rationalization of sin, will even the church of Jesus Christ fail to call sin what it is? Will we join the ranks of those who would make people *pathetic* rather than *guilty?* Where in scripture is sin spoken of as a sickness or disease? Where no choice is involved neither can there be accountability. This is certainly basic, elementary reasoning and only those seeking sanctuary from personal responsibility and accountability could possibly find issue.

SIN IS A SUBSTANCE
False Concept 2

A revolutionary concept, as far as then-young Christendom was concerned, was conceived in the mind of a budding theologian by the name of Augustine. After an immoral and unstructured past that included many years studying the philosophy of Manes, Augustine turned to the teachings of Christ under Ambrose, a leading scholar of that day.

Most likely searching for an explanation of his former conduct and help in understanding his present shortcomings, Augustine began to formulate the doctrine of *original sin* and what is commonly known today as the *Federal Headship Theory*. Briefly, the Federal Headship Theory states that when Adam sinned he did so in proxy for the entire world. All men born thereafter entered the world replete with a *sinful nature* which was and is the causative source of their sins. Thus Adam's original sin was passed on from generation to generation—from parent to child.

Augustine, however well-intentioned he may have been, began what would become centuries of confusion and misunderstanding over the concept of sin. He taught that sin was fundamentally a *physical* rather than a *moral* problem. He even theorized that children were born in Satan's power because:

> They are born of the union of the sexes which cannot even accomplish its own honorable function without the incidence of shameful lust.[6]

Again, it is highly probable that Augustine's tarnished past had a strong bearing on his teaching. Today we refer to this type of person as a *reactionary*. Although Augustine undoubtedly reacted in the right direction to begin with, his extremes would later cause him (and the church) grave problems. He went on to teach that sexual intercourse was a venial sin (unless the motive was procreation) and the act was always shameful since it was always tinged with passion. Only Christ was born pure since conception took place apart from intercourse.[7] Augustine's teaching provided the ground from which the Puritan movement would later grow.

When we analyze the situation in the Garden of Eden we see that when Adam sinned he became depraved in *two* ways:

1) Morally—his soul disobeyed God
2) Physically—his body began to fail

Augustine and subsequent theologians have, in their expounding of the doctrine of total depravity, failed to distinguish between these two types of failure.

Physical (metaphysical) *depravity*—This gives man the bias or the bent toward being sinful, but is not *in itself sinful.* In other words it is an influence to, but not a cause of sin. This depravity comes by *inheritance,* not choice.

Spiritual (moral) *depravity*—This is what we *do* with our situation. It involves unintelligent responses to influences and suggestions. *This is sin,* but it is *not inherited*—it comes by *choice,* it is *created.*

Men today for the most part acknowledge that it is sin when they make wrong choices. The snag is that they attribute these wrong choices to a "sinful nature" which they receive *physically* at birth. It is a basic fact that everything in the universe is inherently *matter* or inherently *moral.* According to the theory that subsequent to Adam's fall, sin has inevitably been *transmitted* from parent to child, sin is evidently *matter* or *substance*—a physical factor. With this in mind, let's consider the following argument:

> If I have inherited this sinful nature from Adam, how is this sinful nature passed on to me? In which part of me is this sinful nature passed on? It must be passed on in the physical body somehow since moral character cannot be passed on. "Moral" has to do with choice and a choice cannot be inherited (only the *results* of a choice).
>
> If a choice *can* be passed on, here is a question that must be answered: If two Christians have a baby, is their choice to be passed on to the baby? They are much closer to the baby genealogically than Adam and their characteristics would be the more dominant or stronger.
>
> Many have said in desperation that sin is passed on in the blood. If this were the case, it might prove interesting to isolate some sin in a test tube. We may ask, in addition, what happens to the Christian who is involved in a serious accident and receives blood given by someone who is not a

Christian? If this sinful nature is present in the donor's blood, does the Christian who receives it take on a sinful disposition again? This theory also makes evangelism much easier. All that would be required to convert a sinner would be a simple blood transfusion, using of course the blood of a Christian. One solution might be to close down our churches and open up Christian hospitals. (Incidentally, did you ever wonder why Jehovah's Witnesses don't allow blood transfusions?)

Lewis Sperry Chafer, the founder and first president of Dallas Theological Seminary, tells us, "Men do not now fall by their first sin; they are *born fallen* sons of Adam."[8] It is only fitting that this statement should be followed by a graduate of this same school of thought commenting on the sin of Adam and Eve: "They actually had something added to them—a sin nature. And *that made them sinners.* Since that awful day of infamy, all men have been *born* with that same, sinful nature, and that is the source of our sins."[9]

As mentioned earlier in this chapter, the concept of *causation* glares at almost every turn. We must keep in mind *that which is caused cannot be free,* nor can it be accountable or responsible. Here again we have man in a pitiable situation deserving sympathy rather than judgment. Isaiah Berlin, in his book *Historical Inevitability*, concludes that Determinism means the elimination of individual responsibility:

Nobody denies that it would be stupid as well as cruel to blame me for not being taller than I am, or to regard the color of my hair or the qualities of my intellect . . . as being due principally to my own free choice; these attributes are as they are through no decision of mine. If I extend this category without unit, then whatever *is* is inevitable . . . to blame and praise . . . becomes an absurd activity. If I were convinced that although choices did affect what occurred, yet they were themselves wholly determined by factors not within the individual's control, I should certainly not regard him as morally praiseworthy or blameworthy.

How could we have stooped and acquiesced to these theological and philosophical absurdities which have crept into the Church? The Word of God is to be presented in such a way that "every mouth may be stopped, and all the world may become guilty before God" (Romans 3:19). If I am born with an *inability* to obey God, then can you conceive of a better excuse for not obeying Him? If I can't obey God, then why should I be disturbed that I'm not obeying Him? Yet the Word of God declares emphatically that *all men are without excuse!* This indicates that all men are *responsible* for their own choices, which implies they are *free to make their own choices.*

> If I was born with an inability to do what God says, how can we justify eternal punishment with the love of God?[10]

This dilemma is readily discerned by some, but the great majority try to ease the pressure and present God's justice by viewing His intention in sending Christ to let all "off the hook" who would respond to His call. The flaw in this argument is that it destroys the aspect of grace (getting something we don't deserve) in Christ's advent by virtue of the fact that, according to this position, God was under *obligation* to send Christ to assure all men a "fair shake."

The Federal Headship Theory, which we have briefly discussed, is an extremely widespread doctrine which is difficult to explain logically. The important factor, however, is whether or not the Bible will allow the representational theory of transmission of sin. Let's look.

> Then the word of the Lord came to me saying,
>
> > "What do you mean by using this proverb concerning the land of Israel saying, 'The fathers eat the sour grapes, but the children's teeth are set on edge'?
> >
> > "As I live," declares the Lord God, "you are surely not going to use this proverb in Israel any more.

"Behold, all souls are Mine; the soul of the father as well as the soul of the son is Mine. The soul who sins will die.

"But if a man is righteous, and practices justice and righteousness . . . if he walks in My statutes and My ordinances so as to deal faithfully— he is righteous and will surely live," declares the Lord God.

"Then he may have a violent son who sheds blood . . . he will surely be put to death; his blood will be on his own head.

"Now behold, he has a son who has observed all his father's sins which he committed, and observing does not do likewise . . . he keeps his hand from the poor, does not take interest or increase, but executes My ordinances, and walks in My statutes; he will not die for his father's iniquity, he will surely live.

"As for his father, because he practiced extortion, robbed his brother, and did what was not good among his people, behold, he will die for his iniquity.

"Yet you say, 'Why should the son not bear the punishment for the father's iniquity?' When the son has practiced justice and righteousness, and has observed all My statutes and done them, he shall surely live.

"The person who sins will die. The son will not bear the punishment for the father's iniquity, nor will the father bear the punishment for the son's iniquity; the righteousness of the righteous will be upon himself, and the wickedness of the wicked will be upon himself."

Ezekiel 18:1–5,9–10,13–14,17–20 (NASB)

The various biblical words used to describe human sin leave absolutely no doubt whatsoever as to sin's true nature. We search in vain for any evidence that would indicate that sin is a substance or anything other than a wrong moral *choice*. We will further pursue the matter of biblical vocabulary later in this chapter.

SIN IS A SLIP
False Concept 3

There are a great many evangelists, Sunday school teachers and pastors who convey an almost accidental picture when they describe the tragedy of Adam and Eve's disobedience in the Garden of Eden. The way the story is often told, we find a couple walking in tender loving fellowship with God, and then, all of a sudden *falling* into sin. This is certainly a misleading word. I personally cannot recall having ever *purposely* fallen. The implications of the term *"the fall"* are certainly less arresting than would be the case with, say, *"the rebellion."* The idea that it is possible to simply slip and fall into sin must be dispensed with all rapidity lest we find ourselves clouded by its influence.

It is important to refresh our memories as to the difference between what transpired in the Garden and a legitimate mistake. We determined earlier that an individual's intentions were examined by the courts in order to ascertain whether or not his actions were *willed*. If the action was *not* willed, then the individual is not dangerous to society. Thus the consequences connected with a murder conviction are far more severe than with a manslaughter conviction because, in the former, there is a premeditated, injurious design involved. Adam and Eve's sin can never be referred to as a slip or ignorant mistake. God gave ample instruction concerning what they were to do and not to do in Eden and included sanctions or consequences to support His words. We read that "the woman being deceived was in the *transgression . . ."* (I Tim. 2:14). We are not dealing with a woman who in her naivete had no understanding of what she was doing, but rather we see a transgressor, one who was *voluntarily deceived,* breaking and violating *known* laws. Then, too, Adam voluntarily transgressed with his wife. I'm persuaded that it would be far more accurate and descriptive if we would refer to the incident in the Garden of Eden as "The Jump"! As Floyd McClung has said, "Every mistake is not a sin, but every sin is a mistake."

SIN IS A SUGGESTION
False Concept 4

Temptation is a universal problem. It is not confined to continents, races or economic classes. Temptation has many faces. It spans the scale from the subtle to the blatant, and seems to have an uncanny knowledge of our susceptibilities. Biblical accounts of temptation range from the well-known flight of Joseph from the seductive advances of Potiphar's wife to the crashing downfall of David with Bathsheba. Compare these to the person who says, "I never have a problem with temptation—I just always give in"!

There are a great number of people who assume that the battery of temptations entering their minds are solicitations of the devil, and their desire to comply emanates from their "sinful nature." This is a common but serious error. God designed human beings replete with many astonishing endowments. Some of these attributes, our emotions, enable us to sense, feel and respond to the thoughts in our mind. Eve's desire for the fruit which her mind perceived as being "a delight" was not a product of any sinful nature. Nor was her desire for further knowledge wrong in itself. There is no necessity of a sinful nature in order to be subject to temptation.

Gordon Olson has given what I consider to be one of the finest definitions of sin:

> Sin is an unintelligent abuse of God-given endowments of personality.[11]

With this definition in mind, let us remember that it is God who has made us the way we are. It is God who has created appetites and desires within us. It is God who formed our emotions to respond to what our minds contemplate. There is no sin in desiring to fulfill or gratify a God-given appetite. Sin enters the picture when we abuse our endowments by trying to gratify ourselves in an *illegal manner* or *proportion*.

Thoughts should not be classified as sin either. It was necessary for Jesus to have comprehended the words of the devil in order for it to have been a legitimate temptation.

Again, *things* cannot be evil and sinful for they are the product of God.

> All things were made by him; and without him
> was not any thing made that was made.
>
> John 1:3

If we respond to temptation by treating it as though it were sin or indicative of sin, then we are forced into the uncomfortable position of considering Jesus an ally in sin since He too was subject to temptation. A suggestion or temptation is not in itself sinful. Things in themselves are not sinful, for sin manifests itself in *unintelligent abuse* of an otherwise good thing.

This is especially critical for those who have been suffering under an unnecessary load of condemnation because they have been tempted. When confronted with a strong desire, it is essential to take hold of the thought and give it a long, analytical look. Then ask yourself if it is possible to wisely gratify that desire. Remember, God does not disapprove of pleasure associated with gratification, but He does mind an unintelligent quest for pleasure in order to gratify yourself at the expense of others. It's probably worth mentioning that all so-called "secret sin" is ultimately at someone else's expense. When we realize that God wants us to be happy and fulfilled, then we will recognize His restraints as blessings designed to increase our enjoyment of life.

SIN IS THE STATUS QUO
False Concept 5

In a book on major biblical themes, Lewis Sperry Chafer reveals the following thought:

> . . . every child of Adam is born with the Adamic
> nature, (and) is ever and always prone to sin,
> and . . . it remains *a vitally active force in every
> Christian's life*. It is never said to be removed or
> eradicated in this life. . . .[12]

How interesting that the nation's number one purveyor of stylized selfishness, Robert Ringer, should say a similar thing. . . .

> You will always act selfishly, no matter how vehemently you resist or protest to the contrary, because such action is automatic. You have no choice in the matter.[13]

I remember getting into my car after work and discovering a note taped to my steering wheel. It was an apology from one of the secretaries who'd had a rough day and had made some rather terse remarks. It read in part: "I'm sorry for having snapped at you—please forgive me for *being human*."

Have you ever heard someone say after they did something wrong, "Well, I'm only human"? We are told today that sin is *"only human."* Sin is kind of a natural thing by implication. "It's just my nature." I'm sure you have noticed Christians wearing buttons on their lapels or bumper stickers on their automobiles with slogans like *"Christians aren't perfect—just forgiven"!*

This was the attitude that former President Carter displayed in his *Playboy* interview. Commenting on adultery, he stated: "I've committed adultery in my heart many times . . . this is something which God realizes I will do . . . and He forgives me for it."

Several years ago I was speaking at a youth missionary retreat in the mountains of southern California. I was talking with a camper who had several questions concerning sin. We were sitting on the bunks reading from I John when another young man entered the cabin to hear these words: "Whosoever abideth in him sinneth not. . . ." (I John 3:6) With red-faced indignation, he proceeded to tell me that it was *impossible* to live without sin, that even Christians expect to sin every day in word, thought and deed. I paused for a moment and asked this young man if he believed sin was the most powerful force in the universe. He didn't think so. What was the purpose of Christ's mission? Was it not to set the captives free, to seek and to save that which was lost? Isn't the message of the gospel, the good news, that Jesus has come to *transform* us by the renewing of our minds? He came not just to save us from hell, the penalty of sin, but from that which actually binds us—*our sin itself!*

Why do we preach a message of defeat? Why do we declare a doctrine of continuing bondage? The Bible states:

> Whosoever is born of God doth not commit sin. . . .
>
> 1 John 3:9

> That ye may approve things that are excellent; that ye may be sincere and without offense till the day of Christ.
>
> Philippians 1:10

> And hereby we do know that we know him, *if* we keep his commandments.
>
> 1 John 2:3

> Whosoever abideth in him (Christ) sinneth not. . . .
>
> 1 John 3:6

Where do we get the idea that sin is only natural and human? Whenever a polygraph test registers a lie, it proclaims that sin is not natural! Whenever one feels *remorse, sorrow,* or *guilt* it tells us with eloquence that sin is not natural! To those who are of the opinion that the only thing that separates a Christian from the world is forgiveness, I can only surmise they have little time for the Word of God.

The arrogant slogan "Christians aren't perfect—just forgiven" brazenly flaunted in the face of the world, is more accurately read, "My conduct is similar to yours—only I'm forgiven and you're not!" What joy do you think God derives out of a "relationship" of that sort? Has He expressed in your relationship, or through His Word, that sin is the status quo for a Christian? What is the blood of Jesus Christ worth? Where is the power in the blood? Is it possible that we have actually accepted the fact that the love of God displayed on Calvary is an anemic force compared to the mighty power of sin?

WHAT IS SIN?

In order to effectively deal with an enemy, it is of utmost importance to be thoroughly and accurately briefed on the qualities and characteristics of the foe. That sin is the deadliest of all foes need hardly be debated. With the defeat and elimination of sin, the cessation of war, crime and cruelty would necessarily follow.

> Christianity now has to preach the diagnosis, in itself very bad news, before it can win a hearing for the cure, . . . a recovery of the old sense of sin is essential.[14]

As long as sin remains an elusive, undefined phantom it is no surprise that its victories over humanity continue to escalate.

SIN IS CALCULATED

Sin is a transgression of God's moral law, the intent to live supremely for oneself at whatever the cost. It is a premeditated, calculated choice to live in a manner contrary to your original design. There is absolutely *no ignorance* involved in sin.

> Jesus said unto them, If ye were blind, ye should have no sin: but now ye say, We see; therefore your sin remaineth.
>
> John 9:41

> Therefore to him that knoweth to do good, and doeth it not, to him it is sin.
>
> James 4:17

> If I had not come and spoken unto them, they had not had sin; but now they have no cloak for

> their sin . . . . If I had not done among them the works which none other man did, they had not had sin: but now have they both seen and hated both me and my Father.
>
> John 15:22,24

It is most enlightening to look at the various scriptural words used to describe sin. When the root words are analyzed in the original biblical languages (Greek—N.T.; Hebrew—O.T.), the overwhelming evidence is that man is a rebel *choosing* to violate known requisites. Here is a sampling:

- To act perversely, to twist and distort
- To be stubbornly disobedient
- To refuse to serve God
- To act treacherously or deceitfully
- To be rebellious
- To be lawless, to refuse to conform
- To be obstinate or uncompliant
- To deviate from the right
- To be ungodly, to act impiously
- To be unjust, to refuse to do right.

Does the Word of God describe sin as a *weakness* or as *rebellion?* There are many Christians who derive a certain amount of satisfaction from their sin. Their conscience, of course, refuses to grant peace when they are living in this abnormal condition. The solution to this situation has been a gross rationalization of their conduct and adherence to the soothing concept that they are *unable to obey God!* This is but a calculated act of treachery and deceit in the continuing insurrection against God's standard and authority.

SIN IS CRUEL

The ruthless, defiant, aggressive characteristics of sin that are the headlines of our race will undoubtedly become our epitaph unless the world we live in can be revived. To the ears of the celestial Listener, earth cries . . . and before the eyes of her Maker . . . earth bleeds.

The cruel nature of sin is nowhere depicted more graphically than in the treacherous dealings of King David toward Uriah, the husband of Bathsheba. It wasn't enough for the king to have taken Uriah's wife to satisfy his lust. David, caught in his own web as a result of Bathsheba's pregnancy, sent for Uriah, who had been away fighting for Israel. The idea was to use Uriah's expression of love for his wife to cover up the king's sin. Uriah's integrity, however, was not a factor that David had reckoned with. The loyal soldier slept with the servants at the door of the palace rather than enjoy what his comrades on the battlefront could not.

When David's desperate attempts to urge Uriah to move home with his wife failed (in spite of David's success in making him drunk), the king, driven to cover his sin, finally settled on a surefire plan. The following morning David sent Uriah off carrying his own death warrant. The king's instructions were immediately understood by his military captain, Joab, and the cruel scheme unfolded. Uriah was placed on the front lines of the battle.

The loyal Uriah probably never noticed his own army quietly retreating behind him as he fought with renewed vitality and determination after his privileged audience with the king. Left exposed and alone, Uriah became the target of the enemy. The king, receiving the news of Uriah's death and heaving a sigh of relief, "graciously" allowed Bathsheba time to mourn her dead husband before making her his own property.

After hearing a story like this one, it doesn't require much effort to become incensed and indignant over man's inhumanity to man. If Uriah had deserved such treatment, the Bible account would not have stirred such pathos. We tend to see sin as a cruel and reprehensible phenomenon in proportion to the goodness and innocence of the victim. In light of this, don't you find it mystifying that people, at least Christian people, are not revolted over what sin has done to *God?*

He came unto His own and His own received Him not.

John 1:11

. . . They have forsaken me the fountain of living waters. . . .

Jeremiah 2:13

I have called, and ye refused; I have stretched out my hand, and no man regarded.

Proverbs 1:24

O my people, what have I done unto thee? and wherein have I wearied thee? testify against me.

Micah 6:3

And when he was come near, he beheld the city and wept over it.

Luke 19:41

Often I have pictured God, the Mighty Ruler of the universe, sitting on His throne with His face buried in His hands, weeping. Sitting on that throne is all the incomprehensible power of the universe under absolute control. Yet the adulterous behavior of His beloved touches the heart and feelings of this mighty yet gentle Being and the response causes the hosts of heaven to marvel.

Where is there a more poignant sound than that of Jehovah sobbing? Who will stand by God in *His* hour of grief?

SIN IS CONTINUOUS

Unfortunately the parade of depravity continues to march down the corridors of human history without fatigue. It is but a brief respite when God leaves His weeping over Adam's race to rejoice over an obedient saint. He made them right but they've all gone wrong. The planet is in the hands of a race of rebels who have defiantly snatched their lives away from God. They demand liberation from God's "celestial colonialism."

In the case of the individual who has chosen to live a life of selfishness, no decision or activity subordinate to this wrong motive of heart may be considered other than "filthy rags." No matter how "good" our deeds may seem on a human level, as long as our supreme purpose in life remains unchanged "all our righteousnesses are as filthy rags" (Isaiah 64:6).

Sin is a choice to seek and maintain our happiness supremely in an unintelligent supposition that this is of paramount importance. This state of sin and rebellion persists until exposed in an encounter with the cross of Jesus Christ.

SIN IS CORROSIVE

Sin is a moral cancer and it tends to spread once it starts. It must be recognized as an extremely dangerous, highly active corrosive that eats away at the human personality. The longer sin continues, the less actual control we have over our lives.

The year 1973 was an especially exciting one for me, as I spent the early months with Youth With A Mission in Switzerland. I have fond memories of the impromptu sledding "expeditions" after evening lectures. After bundling up, several fellows would trudge about half a mile to a local slope pulling their sleds behind them. Even though the slope provided an adequate angle for the average sledder to get a full quota of excitement, the winter sky continually covered the hills with extra coats of snow. As a result, the first few trips down the slope were somewhat less than exhilarating. Each successive run, however, compressed the newly fallen snow eventually carving out a "slide" that gradually gained our respect. In time, the slope became so slick and treacherous that nobody could manage to remain connected to his sled. It was then that our tired but happy group knew it was time to turn in. This is precisely the manner in which sin, persisted in, manifests itself. In the end it becomes extremely difficult to slow down the train of accumulated indulgences.

SIN IS CAPTIVITY

As sin carves its moral slide, each time down becomes easier and easier. We find ourselves inundated by *habits*.

> And you were dead in your trespasses and sins, in which you formerly walked according to the course of this world, according to the prince of the power of the air, of the spirit that is now working in the sons of disobedience. Among them we too all formerly lived in the lusts of our flesh, indulging the desires of the flesh and of the mind, and were by nature children of wrath, even as the rest.
>
> Ephesians 2:1–3 (NASB)

Thayer's Greek Lexicon tells us that "nature" in verse 3 is the result of *habit*. God has admonished us to allow our minds to dwell upon only that which is wholesome (Philippians 4:8), because as a man "thinketh . . . so *is* he" (Proverbs 23:7). In other words:

- Our thoughts and choices become actions
- Our actions become habits
- Our habits become our nature and character
- Our character becomes our destiny

The great danger of sin is that we become slaves to appetites and desires without even noticing what is happening.

> Know ye not, that to whom ye yield yourselves servants to obey, his servants ye are to whom ye obey; whether of sin unto death, or of obedience unto righteousness?
>
> Romans 6:16

A sinful nature develops in our lives through habitual self-indulgence and subsequently affects everything we do. Paul mentions this situation and the impossibility of fighting it in our own strength in the seventh chapter of Romans. Thus we concur that though a sinful nature is present, it originates by choice. For example, the junkie bound by heroine addiction cannot help but crave drugs now, but the origin of the addiction began with his choices.

We have discovered that there are certain emotional gratifications in life that are pleasurable. However, since emotions cannot be experienced directly but rather respond to what the mind thinks upon, the mind therefore is *harnessed* to produce thoughts that will result in emotional gratification.

Emotions can be a hard taskmaster, resulting in an abnormal imbalance, and a chaos of personality. This is slavery. This is *captivity*. The freedom that the world proclaims only leads to bondage. There is no reason to secretly envy the men and women of the world.

> But the wicked are like the troubled sea, when it cannot rest, whose waters cast up mire and dirt. There is no peace, saith my God, to the wicked.
> Isaiah 57:20–21

> . . . the way of transgressors is hard.
> Proverbs 13:15

GUILT AND RESPONSIBILITY FOR SIN

In this day no one is left without a cause to champion. Everyone has a matter in need of attention and justice. The world offers plenty of exploitation, deprivation, unhappiness and brutality to go around. But who is responsible for the groanings of the planet? Is it politicians, corporate executives, scientists? Is it a nation, a race, a society?

Here is an interesting adaptation of a parable from the gospel of Matthew:

And then the servants counseled together saying, "It would be much better to pull out those weeds right now rather than wait, but we must obey the master even when he is wrong. In the meantime, let us look about for the enemy who would do this evil thing to our master, who is kind to everyone and doesn't deserve this treatment." So they quietly inquired and made search in all the region round about, but they could find no one. But one of the servants came privily to the chief steward at night saying, "Sir, forgive me, but I can no longer bear to conceal my secret. I know the enemy who sowed the tares. I saw him do it." At this the chief steward was astonished and full of anger. But before punishing him, he demanded of the servant why he had not come forward sooner. "I dared not," cried the servant. "I scarcely dared to come and tell you this even now. I was awake the night the weeds were sown. I saw the man who did it; he walked past me, seemingly awake and yet asleep, and he did not appear to recognize me. But I recognized him." "And who was he, indeed?" asked the chief steward in great excitement. "Tell me, so that he can be punished." The servant hung his head. Finally, in a low voice he replied. "It was the master himself." And the two agreed to say nothing of this to any man.[15]

It is the Church, those who profess the name of Christ, who must hold forth light or the world will surely perish on the rocks of sin. They will be crushed by the tide of their own folly and neglect if the light of the gospel does not penetrate their clouded minds. The sinner must realize and confess that it is *he himself who is fully to blame*. Dr. Menninger declares, "If the concept of personal responsibility and answerability for ourselves and for others were to return to common acceptance, hope would return to the world with it!"[16]

There are those who declare their belief in God and faith in His doctrines and standards, yet live as though He doesn't exist! Those living under great light who refuse to conform their lives to the truth are only sowing their own destruction. *If you do not mean to live a holy life, then God's house is the last place you should be!*

America's greatest revivalist, Charles G. Finney, once uttered these piercing words:

> Men really intend to secure both this world *and* salvation. They never suppose it wise to lose their own soul. Nor do they think to gain anything by running the risk of losing it. Indeed, they do not mean to run any great risks—only a little, the least they can conveniently make it, and yet gain a large measure of earthly good. But in attempting to get the world, they lose their own souls. God told them they would, but they did not believe him. Rushing on the fearful venture and assuming to be wiser than God, they grasped the world to get it first, thinking to get heaven afterwards; thus they tempted the spirit . . . lost their day of salvation and . . . lost the world besides.[17]

> I have spread out my hands all the day unto a rebellious people, which walketh in a way that was not good, after their own thoughts.
>
> Isaiah 65:2

> They did not see fit to acknowledge God or approve Him or consider Him worth knowing. . . .
>
> Romans 1:28 (AMP)

RECONCILIATION

4/ ROADBLOCKS TO RELATIONSHIP

Through Him (Jesus) we may know God truly as Father; through Him, the universal becomes the particular, the imminent becomes the transcendent, the implicit becomes the explicit, always becomes now . . . It was for this purpose–to open up a way for sinners to know God–that Jesus came among us.

Malcolm Muggeridge

And you, that were sometime alienated and enemies in your mind by wicked works, yet now hath He reconciled.

Colossians 1:21

God became a man to turn creatures into sons . . .

C. S. Lewis

If it is true that intimacy is proportional to grief, then certainly the One that fashioned us and knows our "going in and going out" must be brokenhearted.

I am *broken* (Heb. to shiver or shatter) with their whorish heart, which hath departed from me.

Ezekiel 6:9

Mankind has done its best to shatter all expressions of divine love, severing even diplomatic relations with God. Does this shut the door forever on the God-man relationship? Does so skilled a craftsman exist that can sift through the debris of a relationship that once was and visualize the beauty of its original form?

The human situation, although tragic, is not really that complex. In fact we may summarize it as follows:

1) Man does not like God or even want to know Him.
2) But man *needs* God for sustenance and optimum fulfillment.
3) God loves man deeply and wants the best for him.
4) He therefore attempts to win man back to Himself.

WINNING MAN BACK

The phrase "winning man back" perhaps betrays the fact that people are, in a sense, lost property. They are rebels on a rampage, but even a rebel belongs to somebody. Try as he may, one cannot efface the unmistakable markings of a being made in God's image. He has, in a sense, "stolen" his life from God and given it to moral harlotry. He has left the One who made him. He has left the home where he belongs.

Malcolm Muggeridge, long Britain's thorniest and most eloquent conscience, discussed this phenomenon during the fetal stages of his own conversion experience:

> I have never wanted a God or feared a God or felt any necessity to invent one. Unfortunately, I am driven to the conclusion that God wants me.[1]

GOD'S TASKS

It is extremely difficult, if not impossible, to appreciate a *solution* without an understanding of the *problem*. To oversimplify the problems God faced in restoring a ruptured God-man relationship (reconciliation)* is to face the prospect of missing the full impact of His solution (redemption). In order for God and man to once again enjoy a mutual, loving, happy relationship, several obstacles need to be overcome. We'll take a preliminary look at the various problems in order.

---

*To reconcile means to restore to favor, adjust our differences, cause one thing to cease and another to take its place. The reconciliation outlined in the Bible is twofold: 1) between man and God and 2) between man and man (see 2 Corinthians 5:18–20).

First, the one God loved happened to be a criminal on death row, thus making God's initial order of business to find a way . . .

1) *To remove the just consequence of death from a law violater He loves. [the governmental problem]*

The second problem was that man, by virtue of his moral drift, lost his concept of God. He didn't know what God was like or what He thought. God, therefore, in order to restore a mutually happy relationship needed to . . .

2) *Reveal Himself to man. [the personal problem]*

Thirdly, the problem of man's pride. He had been away from God so long he had lost all perspective regarding to his own importance and ability. He was actually under the impression that life revolved around him. Because there could be no meaningful relationship as long as man had this self-centered opinion, it became necessary for God to . . .

3) *Reveal man to himself. [the hypocritical problem]*

Once this was done, man moved back into fellowship, with a complete pardon in hand and the renewed ability to see God and himself. Yet one problem still remained. In order to induce man to terminate his love affair with sin and to prevent the new relationship from reverting to its prior state God had to find the right formula to . . .

4) *Maintain the restored relationship by establishing a powerful sin-deterrent barrier. [the motivational problem]*

This is part of reconciliation. If and when God found a solution to these problems, the tender love relationship originally intended between God and man, and temporarily enjoyed in Eden, would once again flourish. It is very important at this stage to reiterate that there were *many* things to be accomplished by the atonement. A solution to just one or two of the above problems would not have been adequate. Many theories on the atonement deal with only one or another of the various problems of reconciliation; and while they may deal correctly with that particular aspect, they nevertheless fall into error by not embracing the full design of God in the atonement. The moral influence theory (Socinian), for example, while dealing with the problem of *maintaining* a restored relationship, does not adequately address God's *governmental* problems in the matter of reconciliation.

While any correct, biblical explanation as to the nature of the atonement will include a solution to several objectives, God's design is often such that many ends are accomplished by a solitary action. God did not generate light, for example, only that we might see. While it is true that *without* light we would be totally incapable of viewing our surroundings, there are, as Albert Barnes notes, "numerous other ends known to us, and perhaps many which are unknown, that were equally contemplated in its creation."[2] It is directly responsible for color, warmth and time, as well as being indispensible in the development of agriculture. Many ends, one solution.

Keeping all this in mind, we will now examine in more detail the four major difficulties God faced in His effort to restore the God-man relationship.

GOD'S LION'S DEN
—The Governmental Problem—

Several thousand years ago an incident occurred in the Persian empire revealing a king's dilemma. The king was Darius the Great, whose kingdom extended over much of the civilized world at that time. The administration of the kingdom was handled by a hierarchy of 120 princes who in turn answered to three presidents, of which Daniel was chief. The empire was plagued with political infighting spurred by jealousy, a malady which often accompanies power. Because of Daniel's wise and conscientious leadership, he gained the royal preference, which generated two attitudes in the ranks of David's fellow administrators. The first was spite, in that David was preferred, and the second was a sense of difficulty, because it was not easy to ensnare a faithful and and conscientious man. Finally these evil governors enticed Darius to sign a decree which in essence stated that no one in the kingdom was to petition any man or god other than the king for thirty days. The sanction for disobedience was the lion's den and the decree would stand firm "according to the law of the Medes and Persians, which altereth not." The stage was now set for the downfall of Daniel, the Jew who prayed regularly to the God of Israel.

Daniel's enemies wasted no time in approaching Darius with the reports of their spies. Suddenly the powerful monarch of the Persian empire found himself bound and rendered helpless by the words of his own mouth.

> Then they answered and spoke before the king, "Daniel who is one of the exiles from Judah, pays no attention to you, O king, or to the injunction which you signed, but keeps making his petition three times a day." Then, as soon as the king heard this statement, he was deeply distressed and set his mind on delivering Daniel; and even until sunset he kept exerting himself to rescue him.
>
> Daniel 6:13–14 (NASB)

Darius found himself in the middle of the same governmental dilemma God faced with man. How does a government balance justice and mercy and wisely dispense their consequences for the good of society? The purpose of the laws and courts of our land is justice, not mercy. Every just penalty the lawbreaker pays strengthens moral government; almost every mercy he receives weakens justice, unless government finds a method of blending mercy and justice. Only the gospel can reconcile the two concepts without damaging or misusing one or the other. Had Darius been able to figure out the answer to his dilemma, he would have had to go to the lion's den for Daniel. He loved Daniel, but not that much.

How would you feel if you turned on your radio and heard the news commentator announce that the President of the United States had just issued a blanket pardon to all of America's prison inmates? When the prison doors swung open, what message would be written across the face of each prisoner? *"You can break the law and get away with it!!"* Thus, what happens to the law? What happens to the integrity of the lawgiver?

God could never sacrifice the welfare of His government in such a manner. Knowing full well that law without consequences is merely *advice*, He had to find a viable way to demonstrate to every moral being His *respect* for the law. Compromise on an issue of such immense importance was simply out of the question. God would remain just and righteous in His solemn responsibility to hold the moral fabric of His kingdom intact.

An expansion of God's governmental problem (how to remove the just consequence of death from a law violator whom he loves) reveals the following dilemma:

1) Man had sinned, violating God's moral law.
2) The consequence of this violation was death.
3) Yet God loved his creation and did not want to see him die.

His problem was to find a way to: 1) *uphold His law*, 2) *show His hatred for sin*, 3) *set the man He loved free without encouraging others to sin*.

GRIEF AND WRATH
—The Personal Problem—

In order for humanity to be reconciled to God, it is necessary to know God. We obviously cannot be joined to someone we do not know. We need to know what his character is like, how he is disposed toward us, and how *he feels* concerning sin. We must further take time to study God's love memos dealing with his thoughts and attitudes or be destined as a result of our moral drift to misinterpret Him entirely.

An earlier chapter mentioned the profound alteration

which took place in Adam's heart following his sin. Adam's new desire to conceal himself from God indicated that he believed that God, also, had changed. This very concept has carried on throughout the entire race of rebellious men and women. They imagine a God of wrath filled with a desire for vindication. They wonder if perhaps the wrath of God kindled by their sin may not be, at least partially, appeased by gifts or by suffering. The tragic spectacle of men worshiping God from fear is heightened by pitiful rituals of self-inflicted torment. The worldwide hope is that God will be soothed as He watches the sinner suffer. P. P. Waldenstrom in his book, *Be Ye Reconciled to God*, states:

> Many dear children of God view this as the very essence of Christ's work. They think they never can escape the wrath of God, unless it has been poured out upon someone else in their stead. In their opinion, the chief significance of Christ is that He be a shelter to shield against God or, so to speak, a lightning rod for His wrath, in order that they may feel safe before Him.[3]

Isaiah Watts' hymn highlights this misconception:

> Rich were the drops of Jesus' blood
> That calm'd his frowning face,
> That sprinkled o'er the burning throne
> And turn'd the wrath to grace.
>
> Thy hands, dear Jesus, were not arm'd
> With a revenging rod;
> No hard commission to perform,—
> The vengeance of a God.
> But all was mercy, all was mild,
> And wrath forsook the throne,
> When Christ on the kind errand came
> And brought salvation down.

> As Albert Barnes rightly observes, "In such language as this, while something may be set down to mere poetry and to the overflowing emotions of gratitude to the Saviour for the part which he has

> performed in the work of redemption, it is un-
> doubtedly implied, by the fair interpretation of the
> language, that a *change* has been produced in God
> by the work of the atonement; that in some way a
> Being before stern, severe, and angry has been
> made mild, forgiving and kind."[4]

This serves to illustrate the tremendous need to discuss God's attitude and approach in the process of reconciliation. Christians have grasped hold of scriptures pertaining to God's wrath and, in the midst of their theorizing, missed an extremely important point. It was not *God* who needed to be reconciled to man, but it was *man* who needed to be reconciled to God. God's disposition of love toward man has never changed; it has not been diminished by the "fall" or any other subsequent event. There is, in fact, no sin which man could commit capable of severing God's love. There is nothing one can do to make God stop loving. God hates sin but not people. The love of God never needed to be restored by propitiation, because *it was never lost.* The atonement could not have changed God, for He tells us plainly that His character is unchanging (James 1:17).

> The essential idea in the atonement is, not that
> God was originally stern and inexorable and that
> he has been made mild and merciful by the atone-
> ment, but that the atonement itself has its founda-
> tion in his willingness to pardon; not that he has
> been made benevolent by the atonement, but that
> he was originally so disposed to show mercy that
> he was willing to stoop to any sacrifice but that of
> truth and justice in order that he might show his
> willingness to pardon the guilty. He gave his Son
> to die, not that he might be *bought over* to love,
> but as the *expression* of love.[5]

When the Bible speaks of the wrath of God, to what does it refer? Everywhere the *object* of God's wrath is described as *sin* and *unrighteousness.* This is a hatred that will never be appeased or changed. Christ's death in no way affected the righteous wrath of God toward *sin.* How would the universe survive if God should cease to hate sin?

The Bible also speaks of a "wrath to come" (Luke 3:7). Man's *preparations* for that day are also included in Scripture:

> But, after thy hardness and impenitent heart, treasurest up unto thyself wrath against the day of wrath and revelation of the righteous judgment of God.
>
> Romans 2:5

The first time the word wrath appears here, it may be interpreted to read *guilt*. The second time it appears as the painful duty of a righteous God. It is the consequence levied against unrepentant sinners. We have already seen the incredible grief that sin brings to God, and the execution of judgment brings Him even less comfort. God pleads with men to change their hearts so He can withhold judgment.

> Say to them, As I live, says the Lord God, I have no pleasure in the death of the wicked, but that the wicked turn from his way and live; turn back, turn back from your evil ways; for why will you die; O house of Israel?
>
> Ezekiel 33:11 (RSV)

> For He does not afflict willingly, or grieve the sons of men.
>
> Lamentations 3:33 (NASB)

> Come now, and let us reason together, saith the Lord: though your sins be as scarlet, they shall be white as snow; though they be red like crimson, they shall be as wool. *If ye be willing* and obedient, ye shall eat the good of the land: but if ye refuse *and rebel, ye shall be devoured with the sword: for the mouth of the Lord hath spoken it.*
>
> Isaiah 1:18–20

We can clearly see that it is not God's *desire* to send judgment and if we, like Nineveh, will be willing to repent, then we will find "a gracious and compassionate God, slow to anger and abundant in lovingkindness, *and One who re-lents concerning calamity"* (Jonah 4:2).

On the other hand, if we staunchly *refuse* God's offer to "reason together," there will eventually come a time when God is regretfully conscious that the means at His disposal to secure man's obedience have been exhausted. It is at this moment that God's grief reaches a climax, for He knows that for the highest good of all involved He must judge the unrepentant offender. There is a song on a children's album that expresses this point beautifully, about Noah entering the ark and God's subsequent judgment of wickedness on earth:

> But as the Lord was speaking, He then began to cry. He wept and wept for 40 days. He wept 40 nights. Though it had never rained before in all the earth's long years, now up the ark began to rise upon God's tears.[6]

TWO TYPES OF JUSTICE

We often hear the statement, "God is a God of love but He is also a God of justice." What is wrong with this statement is the obvious error that it equates God's justice with all that is negative. It makes God's justice appear as the inverse of His love. God's justice, on the contrary, is a product or an attribute of His love. It is not and will never be in any way divorced from His benevolence.

It must be remembered that the primary function of law is to secure the happiness and well-being of any given society. Laws are never intended as ends in themselves, but as *means* to an end. Laws can be replaced or dispensed with only if, in so doing, the end which they uphold is not damaged.

An effectual substitute for the normal execution of the penalty for lawbreaking is what King Darius labored earnestly but failed to find. God, on the other hand, *was* able to provide an adequate substitute and satisfy the demands of public justice. An exception would be made and a pardon granted. The biblical word for this substitution is *atone-*

ment. God's solution to His "lion's den" problem was the governmental substitution of the sufferings of Christ for the punishment of sinners.

RETRIBUTIVE JUSTICE	PUBLIC JUSTICE
Looks calculatingly at every individual's situation and exacts strictly in accordance with the deed. The style is "an eye for an eye, a tooth for a tooth." There is *no mercy* and *no pardon* shown where retributive justice is concerned. Most of the time retributive justice cannot be strictly satisfied.	Is basically concerned with the overall interests of the public. Justice is administered with the highest good of those involved as its end. Penalties are executed unless something else is done that will be equally effective in securing the public interests. Public justice regards the spirit of the law instead of the letter of the law.
Forgiveness: Never granted	*Forgiveness:* Permissible—if done wisely

It is crucial to our discussion of reconciliation that we *do not confuse these two types of justice.* If this *does* occur it will thoroughly confound our understanding of the nature of forgiveness.

THE NATURE OF FORGIVENESS

The assertion that Jesus *paid* for our sins has caused confusion within the body of Christ. It is casually accepted that our salvation hinges on a legal transfer of some sort between two members of the Trinity—Jesus and His Father. This has become the nearly unanimous answer to the question, "Who did Christ pay?" If Christ indeed *paid* the Father for sin then it was *retributive justice* that was served and not public justice. We should remember that under retributive justice *no forgiveness is possible.* Forgiveness, correctly defined, is *the relaxation of a legitimate claim.* According to this definition God could not have, as one hymn puts it, *"paid* the debt and *forgave* Me all my sin."

Let me illustrate: If I borrow one hundred dollars on the condition that it be repaid at a later date, the lender has a legitimate claim. But when I return the money, the claim against me is not *relaxed* but *fulfilled*. No forgiveness takes place whatsoever. Taking the illustration one step further, let's assume that after borrowing the hundred dollars, I find for some reason that I am unable to repay my debt. A good friend of mine, however, is good enough to offer one hundred dollars in my stead. Again we have the same result. The claim against me has not been relaxed but fulfilled, and similarly no *forgiveness* whatsoever takes place. The Bible teaching on the nature of forgiveness is seen in one of Jesus' parables:

> For this reason the kingdom of heaven may be compared to a certain king who wished to settle accounts with his slaves. And when he had begun to settle them, there was brought to him one who owed him ten thousand talents. But since he did not have the means to repay, his lord commanded him to be sold, along with his wife and children and all that he had, and repayment to be made. The slave therefore falling down, prostrated himself before him, saying, 'Have patience with me, and I will repay you everything.' And the lord of that slave felt compassion and released him and forgave him the debt.
>
> Matthew 18:23–27 (NASB)

The sole reason for the slave's release was his lord's *compassion*. Forgiveness in this parable is certainly the relaxation of a legitimate claim. No third party intervened, no bargain was made, the debtor was simply *released* from his debt. It is possible to receive payment on a claim, and it is permissible to forgive a claim, but *you cannot do both!* The Bible portrays a God who is completely desirous and willing to forgive sin without receiving any payment to satisfy a vindictive urge.

Elaborating on the subject, Dr. Nathan Beman states,

> "The existence of the attribute of mercy was, like

God Himself, eternal; and no new and superadded motive was necessary in order to elicit this
attribute in action. The atonement was operated
not as a bribe, or reward, or original cause, influencing the divine feelings; nor as a moral per-
suasive to the exercise of compassions hitherto un-
felt; but it opened a channel in which existing af-
fections might freely flow; and, at the same time,
it rendered the pardon and salvation of the sinner
consistent with every principle of the divine government—and every attribute of the divine nature. In one word, the atonement was not the pro-
curing cause of mercy, but it was the mode in
which mercy was to find for itself an illustrious
expression in the system of the Gospel."[7]

One school of thought states that the atonement totally
satisfied retributive justice (the so called satisfaction doctrine). If this is true, then we face the prospect of a divided
Trinity, the second Person of the Trinity being more loving
that the first! Biblical scholar Gustaf Aulen shares Augustine's early concern over this concept.

... He seems to intend a pointed rejection of any
such idea. He denies that God the Father can be
in any way 'placated' by the Son's death; for in
that case there would be a difference of some
kind, even a conflict, between the Father and the
Son: but that is unthinkable, for between the
Father and the Son there is always the most perfect harmony.[8]

The strongest implication of this doctrine, however,
ought to make us shudder. *If* God demands repayment for
what sin was done to Him—*if* He requires full, vindictive
satisfaction before releasing His claim—we find ourselves
facing the conclusion that there is *no loving moral Being in the
universe!* Fortunately this is not the case. The Bible explains
God's purposes in the death of Christ.

Being justified as a gift by His grace through the
redemption which is in Christ Jesus; whom God

> displayed publicly as a propitiation in His blood
> through faith. This was to demonstrate His righ-
> teousness, because in the forbearance of God He
> passed over the sins previously committed; for the
> demonstration, I say, of His righteousness at the
> present time, that He might be just and the jus-
> tifier of the one who has faith in Jesus.
>
> Romans 3:24–26 (NASB)

Jesus' death was a *public demonstration*. This type of public demonstration was the substitute God needed in order to satisfy public justice, since public justice did allow for pardon. This public demonstration of the sufferings of Christ solved God's *governmental* problem by revealing the Lawgiver as *just* and wise in dispensing with the penalty. At the same time, it allowed Him to do what His heart really wanted to do—forgive the offender He loved.

VIRTUOUS LOVE

Virtuous, unselfish love is totally foreign to our way of thinking. Robert Ringer gives his advice on how to be a truly "giving" person.

> Simple reasoning tells you that you must regard
> the interests of others in order to obtain your ob-
> jectives. Fellow human beings represent potential
> values to you in business or personal relation-
> ships, and the rational individual understands that
> to harvest those values he must be willing to fill
> certain needs of others. In this way, the most ra-
> tionally selfish individual is also the most 'giving'
> person.[9]

Lest this should be construed by some convoluted thought process to be Christian love, Ringer scrapes off all semantic frosting and blurts out,

> Don't do something for the reason that it's 'the

right thing to do' if there's no benefit to be derived from it.[10]

This dearth of understanding as to the nature of virtuous love is nowhere manifest as openly as in the contemporary evangelistic altar call. The modern-day evangelist
may lack theological polish, but the really important ingredient for success comes in another package. He must be
able to *sell*. We are living in the era of the pragmatic sermon. Don't analyze its moral content, the question is: *Does
it work?* The rookie evangelist may hone his techniques by
studiously observing automobile salesmen at their best on
late-night television. The next evening salvation is offered
as "the deal of a lifetime." "Ladies and gentlemen, just look
at these extras! He comes to *you*, eagerly waiting to save *you*
from hell and give *you* heaven in return. And if that's not
enough, consider the fact He brings *you* peace and joy for
your present enjoyment. Also for *your* comfort, He will heal
your body, *your* finances, *your* grades—anything *you* need is
available and at the disposal of those who will but believe."
The final pitch sounds something like this, "You can enjoy
all of this at absolutely no extra cost—that's right, no extra
cost. And Jesus Christ is the only One who can make your
life the envy of your friends, so hurry down the aisle today
while the offer lasts!"

From the *very beginning*, people learn that there is no
cost involved in salvation. Jesus is presented to us as *our
servant*, rather than *our Lord*. All that appeals to our self
interests is highlighted so that our reaction to salvation becomes a purely selfish exercise. This is nothing less than a
humanistic invasion into Christianity.

When all of our thoughts of salvation center on the
question "How do I come out?", is it surprising that we
view God's role in reconciliation in the same light? Contrary
to warped speculation, God was never worried about receiving some personal satisfaction for the hurt that peoples'
sin had caused Him. God's love is purely virtuous. It is unselfish, *agape* love. Out of this mysterious love flows God's
only concern, "How will *they* come out?"

THE PROBLEM OF MAN'S PRIDE
—The Hypocritical Problem—

God's *ultimate* objective in the atonement was not rescuing souls from hell, but the restoration of a ruptured relationship. Jesus came to this earth to "seek and to save that which was lost." What was lost? The intimate God-man relationship. From what were we lost? We were lost from the truth of God.

> All of us like sheep have gone astray, each of us
> has turned to his own way. . . .
> Isaiah 53:6 (NASB)

Humanity has left God and in the process has "become vain in (his) imaginations." Apart from God, men lose all sense of proportion about their own importance. Their subjective and superficial opinions about themselves are grossly inflated. But this is no astonishing revelation; one need only look at the faces of the men and women who surround us exuding arrogance in every conceivable setting. The global megalomania of earthlings must stand out in conspicuous absurdity as the vast host of heavenly beings survey God's handiwork.

How can God relate to man in intimate fellowship when man thinks he's something more than he is? Can reconciliation occur while man is preoccupied with the false opinions he has created? The answer is, of course, *no*.

If God and man are going to get together, something must *humble* man so that he is willing to dispense with hypocritical facades. Before reconciliation can occur, we must come to the place where we see ourselves for what we really are.

> I say to every man among you not to think more
> highly of himself than he ought to think; but to
> think so as to have sound judgment. . . .
> Romans 12:3 (NASB)

As blessings tend to increase our concept of our own importance (i.e., salvation, gifts, ministries), God, in order that

He not add to our moral delinquency, must humble us in order to bless us. He must reveal us to ourselves.

A CHANGE THAT LASTS
—The Motivational Problem—

The Bible tells us that people estranged from God are totally and completely corrupt. It is not a matter of cleaning up this sin or that one. Our *whole personality* is enslaved. We have involved ourselves in a life of total bondage.

> Because the mind set on the flesh is hostile toward God it does not subject itself to the Law of God, for it is not even able to do so.
>
> Romans 8:7 (NASB)

How do you deal with a lifetime of learned selfishness and its myriad manifestations? How can you maintain a relationship against the magnetism of former, inflamed appetites and habits? The key is the *mind*. A total *change of mind* is the necessary objective to be achieved in the process of reconciliation. A transformation simply must take place in our thinking. Summing it up, C. S. Lewis stated, "God became man to turn creatures into sons . . . for mere improvement is no redemption . . ."[11]

> And do not be conformed to this world, but be transformed by the *renewing of your mind*, that you may prove what the will of God is, that which is good and acceptable and perfect.
>
> Romans 12:2 (NASB)

MAN HAS NO "ACES"

There is a story in the Old Testament which gives us a glimpse of the amazing role God plays in the process of reconciliation. It is the account of the prophet Hosea.

The Lord said to Hosea, 'Go, take to yourself a

wife of harlotry. . . .' So he went and took Gomer the daughter of Diblaim, and she conceived and bore him a son. And the Lord said to Him, 'Name him Jezreel'. . . . then she conceived again. . . . When she had weaned Lo-ruhamah (a daughter), she conceived and gave birth to (another) son. And the Lord said, 'Name him Lo-ammi. . . .'

Hosea 1:2–9 (NASB)

Later, in a tragic heartrending conversation with his son Jezreel, Hosea offers his lament:

Say ye unto your brethren, Ammi; and to your sisters, Ruhamah. Plead with your mother, plead: for she is not my wife, neither am I her husband: let her therefore put away her whoredoms out of her sight, and her adulteries from between her breasts. . . . For their mother hath played the harlot: she that conceived them hath done shamefully; for she said, I will go after my lovers, that give me my bread and my water, my wool and my flax, mine oil and my drink. Therefore, behold, I will hedge up thy way with thorns and make a wall, that she shall not find her paths. And she shall follow after her lovers, but she shall not overtake them; and she shall seek them but shall not find them . . . then shall she say, I will go and return to my first husband; for then was it better with me than now.

Hosea 2:1–7

Then said the Lord to me, 'Go again, love a woman who is loved by her husband, yet an adultress, even as the Lord loves the sons of Israel, though they turn to other gods . . .' So I brought her for myself for fifteen shekels of silver and a homer and a half of barley. Then I said to her, 'You shall stay with me for many days. You shall not play the harlot, nor shall you have a man; so I will also be toward you.'

Hosea 3:1–3 (NASB)

You would think that Gomer the adulteress would seek the favor of the husband she has wounded. Doesn't it seem right that the *guilty party* ought to seek the forgiveness of the innocent? Sadly, the Bible again reveals to us the fact that no man is seeking God. No man is initiating a reconciliation with his God.

> As it is written, 'There is none righteous, not even one; there is none who understands, there is none who seeks for God; all have turned aside; together they have become useless; there is none who does good, there is not even one.
>
> Romans 3:10–12 (NASB)

We, like the adulteress, have nothing but our shame. We have no "aces up our sleeves," nothing to attract God to us. The Bible clearly reveals that as long as our ultimate intention is bent on the pursuit of selfishness, *all* our righteousness is as filthy rags. If only there were some virtues, at least a few alluring qualities to make it easier for God to overlook our liabilities, but there are none.

> 'She forgot me,' declares the Lord. 'Therefore, behold, I will allure her, Bring her into the wilderness, And speak kindly to her.'
>
> Hosea 2:13–14 (NASB)

This is certainly an amazing display of love, of mercy, and of grace! The powerful God of the universe forms the earth, gathers a handful of newly created soil, forms a man and loves him! But the magnificence of the story is that—

> The Word became flesh, and dwelt among us. . . .
> John 1:14 (NASB)
>
> *and*
>
> While we were yet sinners, *Christ died for us*
> Romans 5:8
>
> *saying*
>
> I will call them my people, which were not my people; and her beloved, which was not beloved.
> Romans 9:25

REDEMPTION

5/THE ULTIMATE SOLUTION

If the benevolence manifested in the atonement does not subdue the selfishness of sinners, their case is hopeless.

Charles G. Finney

It is not clear that the father received the sacrifice, not because He Himself demanded it or needed it, but only on account of the divine economy . . . that He Himself might deliver us, in overcoming the tyrants by His power, and by the mediation of His son bringing us back to Himself?

Gregory of Nazianzus

As a result of the anguish of His soul, He will see it and be satisfied; by His knowledge the Righteous One, My Servant, will justify the many, as He will bear their iniquities. Therefore, I will allot Him a portion with the great, and He will divide the booty with the strong; because He poured out Himself to death, and was numbered with the transgressors; yet He Himself bore the sin of many, and interceded for the transgressors.

Isaiah 53:11–12

God's ultimate solution to the complex problem of reconciliation was, of course, the life and death of His Son, Jesus Christ. And as Malcolm Muggeridge observes:

One thing at least can be said with certainty about the crucifixion of Christ; it was manifestly the most famous death in history. No other death has aroused one-hundredth part of the interest, or been remembered with one-hundredth part of the intensity and concern.[1]

The death of Jesus Christ and the events which surrounded it were extraordinary, not in that a man died but rather in *who* it was that died. If Jesus' life had not had a revolutionary significance and notoriety, His death would have gone unnoticed as just another victim of the Roman epidemic.

QUALIFYING TO CONQUER

On several occasions in the New Testament, God declared His pleasure over the manner of life His Son was leading. As a result of His obedience the "second Adam" was able to bring to God's heart what the "first Adam" never did.

This beautiful portrait of Christ's obedience has been marred by the theological concept of *impeccability*. This concept teaches that Christ could not have succumbed to temptation. It is, of course, extremely difficult to explain the nature of a temptation that is impossible to succumb to. That temptation is *no* really honest temptation. The work of God refutes this concept.

> For we have not a high priest which cannot be touched with the feeling of our infirmities; but was in *all* points tempted like as *we* are, yet without sin.
>
> Hebrews 4:15

Jesus' life was intended to serve as an example of how we are to *overcome*. If it was impossible for Christ to have acceded to temptation, then He was surely not tempted in all ways like we are! He could not have served as an example to us since there was nothing for Him to overcome! If Christ could not have succumbed to temptation then he could not have loved us, either, for love is a proper choice between at least two alternatives.

There are those who believe that the essence of the atonement existed in Christ's obedience to the moral law on behalf of sinners. This also is questionnable on several counts:

1) The moral law required the obedience of Christ himself. Had he *not* obeyed, He would have disqualified Himself as an effective substitute.
2) If *He* had obeyed the law as our substitute, then why should *we* be required to obey it?
3) Had Christ *obeyed* for us, then why would God require Him to *die* also, as if there had been no obedience, and then require *us* to repent and obey as well?

The chorus *Amazing Grace* would certainly take on new meaning were this the case. For it is truly "amazing" grace that requires a debt to be paid repeatedly before an obligation is discharged!

MORE PROBLEMS WITH PAYMENT

Various biblical words and phrases convey the idea that a payment was involved in the atonement; "ransom", "redeem", "you are brought with a price", to name just a few. It is imperative to interpret these words in light of the *overall teaching* of the Word on salvation.

The payment theory, which is sometimes referred to as the satisfaction theory,* originated by and large with Anselm of Canterbury. "He clearly taught an 'objective' atonement, according to which God is the object of Christ's aton-

*The background of the Latin (Satisfaction) theory may truly be called legal—although this school of thought has claimed many adherents, not all theological thinkers have accepted this concept. Dr. Gustaf Aulen in the opening paragraph of his classic work, *Christus Victor*, states: "My work on the history of Christian Doctrine has led me to an ever-deepening conviction that the traditional account of the history of the idea of the Atonement is in need of thorough revision." The fruits of Dr. Aulen's study serve to underscore this dissatisfaction with the "traditional account." Gregory of Nazianzus rejects the idea of ransom (from a legal standpoint) altogether; he will not allow that a ransom was paid to the devil, nor yet to God, for, as he says, "We were not in bondage under God." He prefers to use the idea of sacrifice. N. Rashdall, in his book *The Idea of Atonement in Christian Theology*, finds repeated occasion to express his lively condemnation of the phraseology of a transaction with the devil; such a theory is, he says, hideous, and cannot be taken seriously. Similarly, A.E.N. Hitchcock, in an article, "A Modern Survey of the Atonement," distinguishes four main theories. He rates as the least acceptable the *Ransom-Theory*. Of Ritchel, Aulen states, "We know that his estimate of the Anselmian Satisfaction-Theory was the lowest possible."

ing work, and is reconciled through the satisfaction made to His justice."[2] This theory results from his confusion of the difference between an allegory and a metaphor.

An allegory is a story created to portray a spiritual truth. It can be taken *literally* with the details pressed for meaning. A religious metaphor on the other hand, while also meant to convey a spiritual truth, is *not* to be taken in a literal, physical way. "You are bought with a price" is a good example of a metaphor which is very often interpreted as an allegory. Furthermore, in this particular passage the word *price* can be translated *honor*.

> Wherever . . . analogies from legal procedure are employed, they are usually assumed to prove the presence of the 'objective' or 'judicial' view of the atonement . . . there is need, therefore, of the greatest caution in the exegesis of the language used of the atonement.[3]

Christ has not redeemed us by giving His life as a *ransom* for our sins in order that He might release us—for *God never kept man captive in sin*. On the contrary, it was He who wanted to make man free.

> . . . the Scriptures frequently describe the atonement in language of a *figurative* character; and the *literal* construction (interpretation) which has been put upon this language has, no doubt, sometimes . . . misled the honest inquirer. We are informed by the pen of inspiration, that Christ 'hath purchased' the Church 'with his own blood.' Christians are said to be 'bought with a price.' . . . These and many other passages of similar import, are often pressed into a literal exposition, while their figurative character is entirely overlooked. When the Scriptures tell us, that Christ 'hath purchased' the Church, or that believers 'are bought with a price,' they do not intend to teach us that salvation of sinners through atonement is a pecuniary transaction, regulated according to the principles of debt and credit; but that their salvation was effected, in the moral gov-

ernment of God, by nothing less than the consideration—the stipulated consideration of the death of his beloved Son.

To these figurative expressions are superadded others of human origin—such as: "Christ has paid our debt—has answered the demands of the law, and satisfied the justice of God in our behalf." If we say that Christ has paid our debt, it is true only in a *figurative* sense; and can mean no more nor less than this, that the sufferings of Christ accomplished the same purpose, in the divine administration, which would have been accomplished by our rejection and punishment.

'Being justified *freely* by his *grace* through the redemption which is in Christ Jesus.' We need no other proof than that suggested in this passage, that Christ did not pay the debt, or *literally* suffer the penalty of the law for his people. He prepared the way for our debt to be remitted; or in plain language, dispensing with all metaphor, he made it consistent and proper and honorable for sin to be forgiven according to the prescribed terms of the gospel.[4]

The truth is, Christ paid no man's debt. It is true, indeed, that our deliverance is, in Scripture, sometimes called a redemption; and this word refers to the deliverance of a prisoner from captivity, which is often effected by the payment of a sum of money. Christ is also called 'a ransom,' and we are said to be 'bought with a price.' But it must be remembered that these are *figurative* expressions. They are designed to communicate this idea, that as payment of money as the price of liberty is the ground on which prisoners are released from captivity, so the atonement of Christ is the ground on which sinners are pardoned, or set free from a sentence of condemnation. These passages, thus understood, appear intelligible and consistent; whereas, understood *literally*, they would contradict other plain declarations of the Word of God. It is evident, therefore, that these are metaphorical expressions, and were never designed to be taken in a strictly literal sense.[5]

There is a very real sense, however, in which salvation *did* cost something. There was a very high price for the Father to pay. The cost was His Son's life. C.S. Lewis comments:

> It costs God nothing, so far as we know, to create nice things: but to convert rebellious wills cost Him crucifixion.[6]

There is another aspect to this cost factor. It is discovered in the spiritual equation that intimacy is proportional to grief. The more you love someone the deeper you can be wounded. Simply because God deeply loves us and wants us back, and has expressed His willingness to take us back with open arms, does not mean His forgiveness is without cost.

> In the first place, it isn't always that simple to forgive other people. If someone hurts you in a small way and apologizes, it is easy to accept the apology. But the greater the wrong or the injury, the harder it is to forgive. If a husband is unfaithful to his wife but comes back and asks forgiveness, she may be willing to forgive; but the forgiveness will not be an easy or casual thing. It will cost a great deal. It will hurt. For the essence of forgiveness is that you accept the wrong or the injury that has been done to you; you bear the consequences of it without retaliation and without being bitter or resentful.[7]

The danger lies in the redefining of God's *personal effort* and *sacrifice* (in the atonement) to indicate some type of *commercial transaction*. If we accept the premise that Jesus literally purchased our salvation with His blood, this approach not only portrays God as vindictive and bloodthirsty and totally incompatible with biblical forgiveness, it also presents another grave difficulty. If Jesus literally paid for our sins with his blood (a paid debt is no longer a debt), and He died for the sins of the entire world, then we can come to only one conclusion, *universalism*, which means the whole world will be saved. If salvation is basically a legal transaction, then I have *no debt or obligation* remaining and my *ignorance* of this situation would not alter the fact.

An alternative offered by proponents of the Commercial Transaction Theory is that of a *limited atonement*. This view holds the same premise as the universalists, that the atonement was an exact, literal payment for sin, but concedes that not all are being saved. Therefore, the atonement was *not made for all* but was limited to the *"elect."* Since the concept of a limited atonement is conspicuously absent from the scriptures, we can only view this theory as the product of man's *presumption*. This doctrine of election is clearly refuted in the following scriptural revelations:

> For God so loved the world, that He gave His only begotton Son, that *whoever* believes in Him should not perish, but have eternal life.
>
> John 3:16 (NASB)

> And He Himself is the propitation for our sins; and not for ours only, but also for those of *the whole world*.
>
> 1 John 2:2 (NASB)

> Behold, I stand at the door and knock, if *any one* hears My voice and opens the door. I will come in to him, and will dine with him, and he with Me.
>
> Revelation 3:20 (NASB)

their heart

> This is good and acceptable in the sight of God our Savior, who desires *all men to be saved and to come to the knowledge of the truth*.
>
> 1 Timothy 2:3–4 (NASB)

We also have the problem of knowing whether or not we happen to be one of those fortunate enough "elected" to salvation. How dreadful to be commanded to repent under the penalty of death with only the *possibility* that an atonement was made for you.

SUFFERING VS. PUNISHMENT

Adherents to the Commercial Transaction Theory rightly believe that guilty sinners deserve to be punished. The theory falters, however, when it represents Christ paying the Father an equal amount of suffering in His own person that sinners would have otherwise been liable to pay.

But if Christ was *punished* to purchase our salvation:

1) This would require satisfaction of retributive rather than public justice. (Remember *no amount of punishment will render a sinner less guilty*. Guilt can only be *forgiven*, not punished away.)
2) Punishment implies guilt. (It would be *unjust* for God to punish an *innocent* person.)

The difference between suffering and punishment is simply this: One is *involuntary* while the other is *voluntary*. The Bible clearly teaches that Christ *willingly suffered* and died for our sins.

> Therefore doth my Father love me, because I lay down my life, that I might take it again. No man taketh it from me, but I lay it down of myself. I have power to lay it down, and I have power to take it again. This commandment have I received of my Father.
>
> John 10:17–18

> Then saith Pilate unto him, Speakest thou not unto me? knowest thou not that I have power to crucify thee, and have power to release thee? Jesus answered, Thou couldest have no power at all against me, except it were given thee from above: therefore he that delivered me unto thee hath the greater sin.
>
> John 19:10–11

SACRIFICES AND BLOOD

As we consider Old Testament procedures relating to offerings and sacrifices, we learn a great deal about God's method of forgiveness. These offerings and sacrifices can be divided into two categories:

Sacrifices/offerings for *sin*	Sacrifices/offerings for *thanks*
(generally bloody)	(generally bloodless)

Notice immediately that these sacrifices *did not represent a substitutionary suffering* for the sinner. We draw this conclusion for the following reasons:

1) When an animal was offered as a blood sacrifice it was not tortured slowly but was put to death very quickly.
2) No sacrifices could be offered for crimes that deserved capital punishment. Anyone guilty of a capital crime was executed.
3) In the case of poor families, a bushel of fine flour was accepted for a sin offering in place of a blood sacrifice. It is obviously impossible for flour to suffer.

Neither was the *death* of the animal a vicarious payment for sin for several reasons:

1) Again, no sacrifice could be substituted for the life of one guilty of a sin deserving capital punishment.
2) On the Day of Atonement, confession of sin was made while placing the hands on a goat. This goat was later *released*, while another was slain.
3) The atonement is related to the *blood* of the sacrifice—not to the *death* that produced it, but to the *life* that is in it.

The Old Testament system of sacrificial offerings accomplished two important functions. First, the blood sacrifices were especially designed to allow God (according to public justice) to *pass over* the people's sins and set aside the penalty. In order for pardon to be granted under public justice, the normal execution of the penalty which upholds the law, or gives it "teeth," must be replaced with something equally as effective in upholding the law. The sinner needs to see how awful his sin is *in God's eyes* and he must have a realization of his own guilt. All this could be accomplished on a limited and temporary scale through the Old Testament sacrificial system.

When a sinner was ready to offer up a sacrifice for his sins it was necessary, in the case of an animal, that it be *without spot or blemish.* The killing of anything less than perfect would diminish the impact on the beholder. The sacrificial lamb, for example, was to be a picture of *health* and *innocence* prior to slaughter. This was undoubtedly due to the fact, as we mentioned earlier, that our inclination to see sin as a cruel and reprehensible phenomenon is in proportion to the goodness and innocence of the victim. Malcolm Muggeridge recalls his experience at a sheep-shearing in Australia:

> As the lambs looked up with their gentle frightened eyes, it quite often happened that the mechanical shears drew blood. The sight agitated me abnormally, the blood so red against wool so soft and white. Why did I feel as though I had seen it before, long ago? Why was the sight somehow familiar to me? That was it—the sacrificial Lamb, Agnus Dei.[8]

The Bible does not associate blood with death but with life.

> The life of the flesh is in the blood; and I have given it to you upon the altar to make an atonement for your souls: for it is the blood that maketh an atonement for the soul. . . . For it is the life of all flesh; the blood of it is for the life therefore.
>
> Leviticus 17:11,14

It is common in the Bible for blood to represent life. For example, when Jonathan declared to his father that David was innocent, he said, "Wherefore then wilt thou sin against *innocent blood*, to slay David without a cause? (1 Sam 19:5).[9] In the New Testament the words life and blood are often interchangeable.

> The Son of man came . . . to give his *life* a ransom for many.
>
> Mark 10:45

> We have redemption through his *blood*. . . .
>
> Ephesians 1:7

The one means the same as the other. God intended to put a premium on the concept of life through the blood. This was one of the reasons the Israelites were forbidden to eat blood.

Life is a prize of *ultimate value,* and when taken, the sinner is brought to a sobering realization of the significance God places on sin. The combination of the sacrificial lamb's perfection, innocence and death made a profound impression upon both the individual and the nation.

To illustrate the effects of the sacrifice upon the sinner, we will return by way of imagination to ancient Israel. It was typical of many families in those days to keep animals, particularly lambs, as pets. As in our society, the young children grew very attached to their animals.

> One evening as you and your brothers and sisters are running around outside your house, your father arrives to put a halt to the horseplay. After hustling you in for dinner, he snatches up your favorite lamb and ties it inside the door. On most days Dad's arrival is a highlight, but today something must have gone wrong. He's too serious tonight, not like usual when he throws you up on his shoulders and carries you through the door. Tomorrow, you discover, the family is going to the Temple, but what's really great is that lamb gets to go, too!

Early the next morning your mother wakes you up, tells you to clean up and put on your best clothes. The fact breakfast was skipped this morning for the Lord wasn't new, but Dad has never looked so serious . . . so sober. Anyway, your guess is that he's tying the lamb's feet together so he won't get loose in the Temple.

The family is finally on the way; Dad's in front, with the lamb on his shoulders with Mom and all the siblings in tow. Nearing the Temple you notice some of your friends arriving, but Dad won't let you talk to anybody. Once inside the Temple, all you can see are the backs and legs of a forest of grownups. Nobody's talking; they're all just kind of crying and moaning real loud. Every so often a family or group of people press their way through the crowd heading for the door of the Temple.

It's hard to figure out what's happening. You had never really noticed the people's faces the other times. This was the first time, too, that Dad had ever let the lamb come, though many other people had brought theirs before.

After a very long two hours you have crept near the front. Occasionally you can see the priests' legs and bare feet around the altar through a crack in the crowd. The wailing and moaning near the front is almost deafening.

Finally, your family is standing in front of the altar. There is blood all over the ground and splattered on the priests' clothes. While your attention is fixed on all the blood, Dad has handed the lamb over to a priest. After saying something to Dad he lifts his head and speaks again—probably praying. His hands are both resting on the lamb—when you notice for the first time the long menacing knife at the side of the altar.

The lamb anticipates its future with a meek struggle but the leather cords hold firm. After the priest finishes praying he picks up the knife and puts his hand under the lamb's jaw pulling its head back. Horror-struck, you watch the priest plunge the knife into its throat; the blood spills out onto the breast of the lamb, the priest and the altar. After one last spasmodic convulsion the life of your lamb is over.

As the priest spreads the blood around, the reality of the whole gruesome spectacle begins to melt your frozen stupor. Leaving the temple tears flow uncontrollably as you press through other Jewish families awaiting their turn to approach the altar. Nothing was said on the way home.

That evening, Father lifted your little frame off your tear-stained pillow and gently explained as he had to your older brothers and sisters in prior years how a lamb could die instead of you.

One suspects that the child in our story began to grasp how revolting sin is to God after he saw the event in the Temple. There may not have been a thorough theological understanding, but it can doubtless be said that, at least for a while, sin would not be taken lightly by this child.

Blood signifies a *cleansing agent*, not a *peace offering* to an angry God. The blood, when sprinkled on the altar and mercy seat, was a sign to God that men had seen a life taken and that they, like this youngster, had realized the awfulness of sin and were not inclined to hurry out and commit more.

The atonement was in the bloody *realization of God's view of sin* and His law, and in its ability to *humble* the sinner who recognizes his *guilt* and *responsibility*. When man is in this condition, God can pardon him and reconciliation takes place. The atonement becomes the at-*one*-ment.

> And according to the Law, one may almost say, all things are cleansed with blood, and without shedding of blood there is no forgiveness.
> Hebrews 9:22 (NASB)

The word *"almost"* in this verse is a reminder that on rare occasions poor people could bring fine flour as an atoning sin offering. This reinforces the fact that God is primarily looking for a *heart realization*. Though best brought about through blood, it could also be produced through a cost recognition of another sort—such as food-stuff which was life sustenance to poor families. There are many interesting scriptures in the Bible, particularly in the Old Testament minor prophets, which indicate that if there is *no heart realization, no contrition, no impact* on the one who offers a sacrifice, that blood or no blood, it is *not pleasing* to God.

> For I delight in loyalty rather than sacrifice, and in the knowledge of God rather than burnt offerings.
>
> Hosea 6:6 (NASB)

> Since Ephraim has multiplied altars for sin, they have become altars of sinning for him. Though I wrote for him ten thousand precepts of My law, they are regarded as a strange thing. As for My sacrificial gifts, they sacrifice the flesh and eat it, but the Lord has taken no delight in them. Now He will remember their iniquity, and punish them for their sins; they will return to Egypt.
>
> Hosea 8:11–13 (NASB)

> 'I hate, I reject your festivals, nor do I delight in your solemn assemblies. Even though you offer up to me burnt offerings and your grain offerings, I will not accept them; and I will not even look at the peace offering of your fatlings. Take away from Me the noise of your songs; I will not even listen to the sound of your harps. But let justice roll down like waters and righteousness like an ever-flowing stream. Did you present Me with sacrifices and grain offerings in the wilderness for forty years, O house of Israel? You also carried along Sikkuth your king and Kiyyun, your images, the star of your gods which you made for yourselves. Therefore, I will make you go into exile beyond Damascus,' says the Lord, whose name is the God of hosts.
>
> Amos 5:21–27 (NASB)

> With what shall I come to the Lord and bow myself before the God on high? Shall I come to Him with burnt offerings, with yearling calves? Does the Lord take delight in thousands of rams, in ten

thousand rivers of oil? Shall I present my first-
born for my rebellious acts, the fruit of my body
for the sin of my soul? He has told you, O man,
what is good; and what does the Lord require of
you but to do justice, to love kindness, and to
walk humbly with your God?

Micah 6:6–8 (NASB)

Therefore, when He comes into the world, He
says, 'Sacrifice and offering Thou hast not desired,
but a body Thou hast prepared for Me; in whole
burnt offerings and sacrifices for sin Thou hast
taken no pleasure.'

Hebrews 10:5–6 (NASB)

For many the sacrifices had become nothing more than
a tiresome ritual. People grew hard and callous and eventually began to engage in deceit and profiteering in the Temple. As long as there was an absence of heart contrition
there was no efficacy in the sacrifices. Twice Jesus had to
drive out merchandisers from the Temple who were making
enormous profits from animals sold as sacrifices. It was
against this perversion that Jesus burned with indignation.
This practice, however, was nothing new, as we note in the
book of Malachi:

'Oh that there were one among you who would
shut the gates, that you might not uselessly kindle
fire on My altar! I am not pleased with you,' says
the Lord of hosts, 'nor will I accept an offering
from you. For from the rising sun, even to its setting, My name will be great among the nations,
and in every place incense is going to be offered
to My name, and a grain offering that is pure; for
My name will be great among the nations,' says
the Lord of hosts. 'But you are profaning it, in
that you say, "The table of the Lord is defiled,
and as for its fruit, its food is to be despised." You
also say, "My, how tiresome it is!" And you dis-
dainfully sniff at it,' says the Lord of hosts, 'and
you bring what was taken by robbery, and what is
lame or sick; so you bring the offering! Should I
receive that from your hand?' says the Lord. 'But

cursed be the swindler who has a male in his flock, and vows it, but sacrifices a blemished animal to the Lord, for I am a great King,' says the Lord of hosts, 'and My name is feared among the nations.'

Malachi 1:10–14 (NASB)

The difficulty of the sacrificial system was that it was only a temporary solution. The lingering effect of the sacrifice of the little child's lamb lasted for weeks or perhaps months. But eventually the impression wore off and had to be continuously repeated to remind the people of the true nature of sin.

But in those sacrifices there is a remembrance again made of sins every year.

Hebrews 10:3

A person needed a system whereby one could be totally and *permanently* changed from within, a system whereby one's sin wouldn't be merely *covered* but *removed!*

Now let us examine the *second* function of the old covenant sacrificial system. Because man had strayed so far from God and had lost his concept of God, it accordingly became necessary to slowly and *progressively* bring him back to the place of complete fellowship. In other words, the old covenant was a *foreshadowing of an awesome event.* The sacrificial system was to build anticipation, looking forward to the full solution of the problems of reconciliation in the Person of Jesus Christ.

Blood sacrifices *could not* take away sin.	The atonement of Christ *did* take away sin.
And every priest stands daily ministering an offering time after time the same sacrifices, which can never take away sins. . . .	. . . but now once at the consummation He has been manifested to put away sin by the sacrifice of Himself.
Hebrews 10:11	Hebrews 9:26

For it is impossible for the blood of bulls and goats to take away sins.

Hebrews 10:4

The repeated ritual of sacrifices:

1) Cannot make the worshipper perfect in conscience.
Heb. 9:9

2) Can never make perfect those who draw near.
Heb. 10:1

3) Cannot remove consciousness (guilt) of sins.
Heb. 10:2

The one-time, voluntary sufferings of Christ:

1) Cleansed our hearts from an evil conscience (superego).
Heb. 10:22

2) Perfects for all time those who are sanctified.
Heb. 10:14

3) Cleansed our conscience.
Heb. 9:14
and
4) Puts His laws in our hearts and minds.
Heb. 10:16

Then said he, Lo, I come to do thy will, O God. He taketh away the first, that he may establish the second.

Hebrews 10:9

For the law made nothing perfect, but the bringing in of a better hope did; by the which we draw nigh unto God.

Hebrews 7:19

The blood of Christ opened, as the song says, "a new and living way." No longer would we relate to God on the basis of an external set of laws. Something happened to us when we saw Christ die under the weight of our sin. We were won by the love of Christ back into *relationship*. He put His laws in our hearts and minds. We keep them without even thinking about them because we're back in a love relationship!

I think this issue was well captured in a story I've often heard repeated. A young woman in starry-eyed haste married a man who turned out to be a cruel tyrant. He often stayed out late drinking. One thing he faithfully saw to was a daily list of chores and duties which he expected his wife to complete. At the end of the day, if the duties were not accomplished or executed to his satisfaction, he would beat and abuse his wife. In time, this husband died a broken and bitter man. Shortly thereafter, the woman remarried. This time she married a man whose character was diametrically opposed to that of her first husband. He was a gentle, sensitive and loving man who spent many hours holding his wife's wounded personality in his embrace. In time, remarkable emotional healing became manifest. One afternoon, as she went through the house singing and cleaning, she found a scrap of paper wedged in the crack of the sofa. Switching off the vacuum cleaner, she sat down to read it. Slowly tears began to well up in her eyes and trickle down her cheeks. It was one of her previous husband's old lists. As her eyes descended the list, she realized that she was doing everything on it, without being told. No external list was given her each morning. It was written on her heart.

Paul sums up the effect of the new love relationship.

> For by one offering He has perfected for all time those who are sanctified. And the Holy Spirit also bears witness . . . 'This is the covenant that I will make with them after those days, says the Lord: I will put My laws upon their heart, and upon their mind I will write them.'
>
> Hebrews 10:14–16 (NASB)

> The blood of Jesus is no admission fee which God has accepted to let sinners into Heaven; it is the means He Himself has given to sinners to cleanse them from sin . . . Jesus' blood was not shed for the purpose of inducing God to let the unclean stand for the clean; but to make the unclean clean.[10]

It is important when we are discussing the new covenant that we maintain our theological equilibrium. In recent days many castigate the law as if it were the brainchild of Lucifer. Have we so quickly forgotten David's words, "Thy law is my delight"? (Psalm 119:77). "More desirable than gold" he tells us, "Sweeter also than honey." Let us recall Moses' words, "So the Lord commanded us to observe all these statutes, to fear the Lord our God *for our good always* and for our survival. . . ." (Deut. 6:24).

When the Bible talks about an imperfect law and replacement of the old system, it refers to *Ceremonial Law*, not the *Moral Law*. Those who fail to make a distinction here will develop serious difficulties in their lives as well as their theology.

WHAT KILLED JESUS?

This is a most important question if we are ever to fully understand the inner workings of Jesus' atoning death. If it were anyone else's death the question might seem academic. In this case, however, the implications are far too demanding. What other death, for instance, has been remembered with such passion for so long? Martyr's deaths, though perhaps remembered for a time, are prone to fade into the din and expediency of contemporary living. But Jesus was no mere martyr; for while a martyr dies to *support* a cause, the death of Christ *began* a movement that has swept the earth. And while it goes without saying that the blood of martyrs incites and inspires, and is even the seed of the church, who will be so brash as to claim it can forgive men's sins?

What killed Jesus? If the Bible is taken as a reliable source, it was clearly something other than crucifixion. While this declaration is sure to trigger scoffing among casual inquirers, those who take the time to explore will discover the evidence is solid. If, for example, crucifixion is accepted as the cause of death, it follows that Jesus was *mur-

dered; and murder is simply not consistent with scriptural revelation. Murder is the taking of a life, and Jesus' life was never *taken* from him. It was, quite to the contrary, *willingly given* or, in biblical terminology, "laid down." Jesus made this point abundantly clear so that there would be no misunderstanding.

> For this reason the Father loves Me, because I lay down my life that I may take it again. No one has taken it away from Me but I lay it down on My own initiative. . . .
>
> John 10:17–18 (NASB)

The two questions concerning the death of Christ upon which most theologians are fairly well agreed encompass *where* he died, and *when* he died. Few will dispute the fact that Jesus' final physical demise took place while he was suspended from a Roman cross. There is likewise little controversy over the matter of his unusually rapid death. Although Pilate was initially startled by the news of Jesus' early death, he settled the situation by summoning eye-witness verification.

> And Pilate wondered if He was dead by this time, and summoning the centurion, he questioned him as to whether He was already dead.
>
> Mark 15:44 (NASB)

The real issue in question is *how* Jesus died. Here both medical and theological authorities offer varied explanations. While some appear plausible enough, others are weighted with speculation. Disagreement, present not only within the respective disciplines, but between them as well, has at times been difficult to sort. However, in keeping with modern scientific trend, medical "experts" seem to have usurped the last word with increasing consistency by virtue of the sanctity of their empirically verifiable evidence. All theological theories must these days run the scientific gauntlet in order to earn their credibility.

It was unquestionably a fortuitous moment for Christendom when that spear was so precisely thrust into

Christ's defenseless side. Although it is doubtful that any of Calvary's speculators, sympathetic or otherwise, paused to interpret the subsequent flow, today in retrospect when the account is read from John's gospel one gets the distinct impression from his almost impassioned emphasis that it is a clue which will in time bear some noteworthy significance.

> But one of the soldiers pierced His side with a spear, and immediately there came out blood and water. And he who has seen has borne witness, and his witness is true; and he knows that he is telling the truth, so that you also may believe.
>
> John 19:34–35 (NASB)

With one fateful blow the anonymous legionaire opened a channel for physician and theologian alike to gaze into the Saviour's heart. For Christians, it merely substantiates what they have intuitively known all along. As for medical men, they shall have their mini-autopsy.

THE SIN BEARER

As the initial phase of God's marvelous plan to reveal Himself to man drew to a close, He raised up a special man. He was called a forerunner to further stimulate man's anticipation of a stunning climax. This remarkable event took place, of course, when:

> the Word became flesh, and dwelt among us. . . . John bore witness of Him, and cried out, saying, "This was He of whom I said, 'He who comes after me has a higher rank than I, for He existed before me.'"
>
> John 1:14–15 (NASB)

This was also the Man of whom the prophet Isaiah wrote:

> He has no stately form or majesty that we should look upon Him, nor appearance that we should be

attracted to Him. He was despised and forsaken of men, a man of sorrows, and acquainted with grief; and like one from whom men hide their face. He was despised, and we did not esteem Him. Surely our griefs He Himself bore, and our sorrows He carried. . . .

Isaiah 53:2–4 (NASB)

He was the humble Servant who came to earth to identify with our situation; the one John recognized from the beginning as *The Sin Bearer*.

The next day he saw Jesus coming to him, and said, "Behold, the Lamb of God who takes away the sin of the world!"

John 1:29 (NASB)

As the drama unfolds, we begin to understand the significance of Isaiah's words: "Surely he hath borne our griefs, and carried our sorrows . . ." What an ignominious scenario!

In the beginning was the Word (Jesus), and the Word was *with* God and the Word *was* God.

He was *in* the world, and the world was made *through* Him, and the world *did not know Him.*

He came to his *own* (Greek—his own things, possessions, domain), and those who were His own *did not receive Him.*

John 1:1,10–11 (NASB)

As Jesus moved about the people He knew so well it hurt that they didn't know *Him*. Christ treasured God's original design for man in His heart and mind, for, though in human flesh, He was as Paul reminds us "the exact representation of His (God's) nature." From the multiple marriages of the woman of Samaria, to the deceit in Jerusalem's marketplace, to the rotting flesh of Lazarus, the unnatural perversions of sin must have begun to weigh on the soul of The Sin Bearer.

And when evening had come, they brought to Him many who were demon-possessed; and He cast out the spirits with a word, and healed all who were ill; in order that . . . (it) might be fulfilled, "He Himself took our infirmities, and carried away our diseases."

Matthew 8:16–17 (NASB)

And they brought to Him one who was deaf and spoke with difficulty. . . . and looking up to heaven with a deep sigh, He said to him, "Ephphatha!" that is, "Be opened!"

Mark 7:32,34 (NASB)

When Jesus therefore saw her weeping, and the Jews who came with her, also weeping, He was deeply moved in spirit, and was troubled, and said, "Where have you laid him?" They said to Him, "Lord, come and see." Jesus wept.

John 11:33–35 (NASB)

And he sighed deeply in his spirit and saith, Why doth this generation seek after a sign? verily I say unto you, There shall no sign be given unto this generation.

Mark 8:12

O Jerusalem, Jerusalem, thou that killest the prophets, and stonest them which are sent unto thee, how often would I have gathered thy children together, even as a hen gathereth her chickens under her wings, and ye would not!

Matthew 23:37

And when he was come near, he beheld the city, and wept over it.

Luke 19:41

Although it has been many years since grief was openly recognized as a cause of death, a growing number of physicians are once again giving attention to the relationship between various sociopsychological factors and heart disease. Dr. James J. Lynch in his highly acclaimed book, *The Broken*

Heart, states, "Stress, pain, anxiety, fear, and rage sometimes appear in indexes of textbooks on the heart, but never *love*." And yet, "In a surprising number of cases of *premature* coronary heart disease and *premature* death, interpersonal unhappiness, the lack of love, and human loneliness seem to appear as root causes of the physical problems . . . We have learned that human beings have varied, and at times profound, effects on the cardiac systems of other human beings." Lynch goes on to say, "Loneliness and grief often overwhelm bereaved individuals and the toll taken on the heart can be clearly seen. As the mortality statistics indicate, this is no myth or romantic fairy tale—all available evidence suggests that people do indeed die of broken hearts."[11] Grief researcher Colin Parkes notes in his book, *Bereavement*, that in seventy-five percent of the cases studied, the cause of death in bereaved individuals was coronary thrombosis or arteriosclerosis.[12]

Dr. Arthur Brown of the University of Texas has been involved in extensive research on nervous and ionic factors in sudden cardiac death. His findings, acknowledged in more than sixty publications, also strongly suggest a significant relationship between emotional stress and heart disease. Another endorsement of the sociopsychological link to heart disease comes from Dr. C. David Jenkins, who, after reviewing some of the psychological and social precursors of coronary heart disease, stated in the *New England Journal of Medicine*, "A broad array of recent studies . . . point with ever increasing certainty to the position that certain psychological, social and behavior conditions do put persons at a higher risk of clinically manifest coronary disease."[13]

It has been said that grief is proportional to intimacy. The greater degree of knowledgeable love one has toward another, the greater one's potential for being hurt. This is no profound revelation; it is something a great many of us have personally experienced. Hurt or grief, while rare in casual relationships, is often manifest in intimate encounters. Dr. George Engel of the Rochester University Medical School, in a carefully controlled six-year study in which he reconstructed the backgrounds of 170 sudden deaths, was able to document that in a great majority of the cases some type of interpersonal loss preceded the deaths.[14] The high coincidence of grief and loss that surrounded many of the deaths noted by Dr. Engel is striking. Further laboratory experiments involving various cardiac responses in animals to loss and affection, as well as clinical studies in psychiatric wards and hospital shock-trauma and coronary care units, all suggest the human heart is profoundly and sometimes mortally affected by human emotions.

Jesus took it all in—identifying with the sin and sorrow of humankind. Finally the load He was carrying accumulated to the point that He took the disciples aside and said:

> Behold, we are going up to Jerusalem, and all things which are written through the prophets about the Son of Man will be accomplished.
>
> Luke 18:31 (NASB)

> And lifting up His eyes to heaven, He said, "Father, the hour has come. . . ."
>
> John 17:1

His time was at hand. How did He know? I believe His knowledge came from deep within, perhaps regulated by the pressure upon His heart. And it was this inner knowledge which told Him His heart was at the straining point. He would soon undergo, as the French physician Pierre Barbet describes,

> An appalling mental agony, produced by the foreknowledge of His physical Passion, and the knowledge of all the sins of men, the burden of which He was Himself assuming for their redemption. He Himself had said to the Apostles: 'My soul is exceedingly sorrowful, even unto death.' Such deep distress can bring on a phenomenon which is known to medical men. This phenomenon, which is also extremely rare, is provoked by some great mental disturbance, following on deep emotion or great fear.[15]

This phenomenon to which the doctor refers is, of course, the sweating of blood in the Garden of Gethsemane. Jesus recognized within Himself that He was soon to face that moment for which He had come into the world. This was the moment of truth, the moment of destiny. The climax to which all of God's prophets, covenants and forerunners had led was now ready to unfold its awesome drama on Calvary.

As Jesus took the sins of the whole world deep into his heart and mind, the anguish of His soul reached unbearable proportions when, for the first time in eternity, there was a breach in the fellowship of the Trinity. We hear the lonely wail of One who recognized the full terror of sin.

> And at the ninth hour Jesus cried out with a loud voice, "Eloi, Eloi, lama sabachthani?" which is translated, My God, My God, why hast thou forsaken Me?
>
> Mark 15:34

Finally the increasing weight of our sin could be borne no longer and Jesus, who had identified so long with us, *died of grief* with a *broken, heavy heart!*

> And He Himself bore our sins in His body on the cross, that we might die to sin and live to righteousness. . . .
>
> 1 Peter 2:24

> *As a result of the anguish of His Soul,* He will see it and be satisfied; by His knowledge the Righteous One, My servant, will justify the many, as He will bear their iniquities. Therefore, I will allot Him a portion with the great, and He shall divide the booty with the strong; because He *poured out Himself to death . . .*
>
> Isaiah 53:11–12

Much of the excruciating agony connected with crucifixion centered on the victim's incessant quest for air. Initially when the nails were pounded into the extremities, the victim was laid out, arms extended, at a 90 degree angle parallel to the crossbeam. But as the cross and its pendent flesh were hoisted into an upright position, the arms with the weight of the entire body dragging on them sagged to approximately 65 degrees. Shortly thereafter the muscles started to contract violently. The cramps began in the forearm and spread to the upper arm and shoulders before moving rapidly into the lower limbs and trunk. Soon the spasms which caused the fingers and toes to curl inward were generalized in a state of tetany. The stomach muscles tightened to form a hollow beneath the grotesquely distended ribcage. The lungs filled with air, but due to the contraction of the expiratory muscles, were unable to expel it. Asphyxiation then began.

The only way to remedy the situation and stave off death was to relieve the drag on the hands and arms which, in Jesus' case, has been estimated to have been nearly 240 pounds per hand. Using the nail through his feet as a fulcrum, the victim was, with considerable effort, able to raise himself to an upright position. This maneuver relaxed the effects of the tetanization in the muscles (at least some of them), unloaded the air trapped in the lungs and avoided asphyxiation. The relief, however, was only temporary and within moments, the victim sunk inevitably into a state of tetanization. This macabre struggle continued until exhaustion prevented the victim from escaping asphyxiation and finally ushered him to death's door.

The Jews had a great dread about the overnight presence of corpses, and this was a particular worry on the eve of the passover. Since few, if any, at the time recognized Jesus as the Paschal Lamb, his presence, along with that of his two fellow victims, was construed in the Holy City as an unclean, not to mention unsightly, nuisance. Accordingly, Jerusalem's rule-keeping power-brokers approached Pilate with the request, as John records, "That their legs might be broken and that they might be taken away" (John 19:31). The breaking of the legs effectively hastened death in that it prevented the victim from pushing up for air. Once this occurred, asphyxiation quickly claimed the unfortunate souls. It was an unpleasant end to an agonizing process.

Ill intent notwithstanding, the snapping of Jesus' bones simply wasn't to be. When the soldiers arrived to end it all, they discovered, probably much to their chagrin, that Jesus had already expired. One legionaire, frustrated that the fun had ended prematurely, and in order to leave an official insignia of death, thrust his lance into Jesus' side as a parting *coup de grace.* Out of the wound, as John's gospel records, flowed "blood and water."

As has already been mentioned, crucifixion was a slow, lingering death that could, in some cases, take a strong man several days to die. Thus, when after only a matter of hours the body of Jesus was requested from Pilate, the Roman governor marveled that Jesus had died so quickly.

He *did not die of crucifixion,* but rather from the *internal agony of His soul.* Crucifixion merely facilitated his death. No man took the life of Jesus. He died as a result of a *voluntary identification,* the sin of the world crushing out His life.*

During a time in Israel's history when the hills surrounding Jerusalem had become a virtual forest of crosses, even the hardened and calloused Roman executioner recognized that he had never seen a man die like this before.

> And Jesus uttered a loud cry, and breathed His last . . . and when the centurion, who was standing right in front of Him, saw the way He breathed his last, he said, "Truly this man was the Son of God!"
>
> Mark 15:37,39 (NASB)

And, as the holy Day of Atonement, the sacrifice had a profound impact on the beholders.

> And all the people that came together to that sight, beholding the things which were done, smote their breasts, and returned.
>
> Luke 23:48

*Crucifixion provided Jesus with the prolonged period of consciousness necessary for His voluntary death. Jesus' conscious identification and death over our sin would have been frustrated had He been drugged (which he refused). In addition, had he been executed any other way—by sword or more likely by stoning, He would have lost consciousness and been murdered rather than "pouring out His soul unto death."

IT IS FINISHED

As Jesus uttered these memorable words, the veil to the Holy of Holies was rent from top to bottom, signifying an answer had been found to history's most complex set of problems. Let us look at how the life, suffering and death of Jesus fully solved the problems of restoring the broken God-man relationship.

One does not solve an *unlovely problem* with a *lovely solution*. That's like sentencing a convicted murderer to a week's work in a florist shop. It doesn't help him and it certainly devastates society. If all we desire to do is protect society, then full punishment is sufficient. But God wanted more than this. He wanted the protection of society and *the reformation of a sinner.*

As Jesus with all His rights to dignity and greatness died in such a gruesome manner, the entire spectacle took on overwhelming impact. This was no mere bleating animal, but the man who had claimed deity, substantiating His claim with remarkable miracles and impeccability. The moral force generated by the life and passion of this Lamb proved to be of far greater intensity than the threat of eternal punishment had ever been.

The account of the Greek king, Zaleucus, is a prime analogy of God's remarkable solution on Calvary. His kingdom plagued with chronic adultery, Zaleucus issued an edict that anyone caught in the act would lose their eyesight. The result was a dramatic and immediate halt to the epidemic of infidelity. Then with a tragic twist of irony, the King's son was indicted as the initial violator of the new edict.

After wrestling with the situation, in much the same way as his historical predecessor Darius, the king made his decision. Assembling the people together King Zaleucus, in the audience of his subjects, proceeded to put out one of his son's eyes and then—one of his own. In this act the king was able to uphold his law, reveal conclusively his hatred of evil, and free the son he loved. In that kingdom *the sight of a one-eyed king was a far greater moral deterrent than a totally blind son.*

In the atonement God revealed Himself to man in the clearest of terms. The Bible tells us that Jesus was an exact representation of God's nature. Jesus states, "He that hath seen Me hath seen the Father. . . ." (John 14:9). The heart of God Himself was lifted up on a cross for the world to behold as He suffered, agonized and finally burst under the weight of man's sins.

It was evidently a new and deeper revelation of the depth of God's love to the host of heavenly beings. This revelation would have been lost had there not been an opportunity for God to pour Himself out in such a manner.

> For God so loved the world, that He gave His only begotten Son. . . .
>
> John 3:16

SUBDUING OR SUPPRESSING?

What then does the crucifixion signify in an age like ours? I see it in the first place as a sublime mockery of all earthly authority and power. The crown of thorns, the purple robe, the ironical title, 'King of the Jews,' were intended to mock or parody Christ's pretentions to be the Messiah; in fact, they rather hold up to ridicule and contempt all crowns, all roses, all kings that ever were . . . look under the crown and you see the thorns beneath; pull aside the purple robe, and lo! Nakedness; look into the grandiloquent titles and they are seen to be no more substantial than Christ's ribald one of 'King of the Jews' scrawled above His cross. . . . It was the sort of incident—a man dying in that slow public way—which must have generated its own immediate tension in the beholders, even though they were unaware of the nature and magnitude of the stupendous drama being enacted before them. In some vague way they expect something to happen, and so it does . . ."[16]

The power of the cross does not lie in some abstract, ethereal, cosmic transaction but rather in a literal subduing of the rebellious human heart.[17] God's desire was never to *suppress* rebels, for certainly that would have been easy enough, but to *subdue* their pride to once again enjoy their fellowship.

The exertion of force, though it results in rapid submission, cannot subdue the heart. Consequently, true fellowship devolves to respect based on fear. *God's ultimate goal has never been to save us from hell.* He came rather to save us from *ourselves*—from our *sin.*

> And she shall bring forth a son, and thou shalt call His name JESUS: for he shall save his people from their sins.
>
> Matthew 1:21

Although it is true that the atonement or substitutionary death of Christ markedly reduces the amount of suffering in the universe, the divine objective was to reveal the true human condition. While it would take a far greater effort to subdue man's heart rather than simply doling out His just deserts, this was the path God chose.

The cross of Jesus Christ thus understood provides an imposing barrier to the individual contemplating sin. To do so he must harden himself against the loving gaze of a suffering Savior as he moves toward each selfish gratification. He must stubbornly ignore the cross as a roadblock, and reject the sacrifice of Jesus.

Jesus was able through his suffering to do what the Old Testament sacrifices never could—provide a lasting, moral force to alter our entire outlook on sin. Perhaps in time the death of an innocent lamb might fade in our minds and be forgotten. But neither heaven nor earth will forget the day God came to earth to wash the feet of His enemies.

> While we were enemies, we were reconciled to God through the death of His Son. . . .
>
> Romans 5:10

REPENTANCE

6/SURRENDER YOUR SWORD

Salvation—Phase One

And the times of this ignorance God winked at; but now commandeth all men everywhere to repent.

Acts 17:30

We are not merely imperfect creatures who must be improved: we are . . . rebels who must lay down our arms.

C.S. Lewis

Repentance is the first bit of firm ground underfoot, the only one from which we can go forward . . . repentance is the only starting point for spiritual growth.

Alexander Solzhenitsyn

Not long ago a movie appeared on television entitled "The Candidate," starring Robert Redford. Although I missed a good portion of the film, I turned the set on in time to catch the rather intriguing conclusion. The setting was inside an enormous arena where a political congregation had come to cheer on their candidates. The place was jam-packed and rippling with energy and anticipation. The viewer was made extremely tense by a periodic scan of the candidates on the platform through the cross-hairs of a scope on a high-powered rifle. Finally, the inevitable occurred as several politicians were felled by an assassin lurking in the rafters.

The ensuing footage captured one of the most unbounded displays of mass hysteria I've seen filmed. Security guards were swept along helplessly in the raging torrent of terrorized humanity. Scores of people were mercilessly trampled to death in the every-man-for-himself stampede.

Heaving officials beaded with perspiration called on Redford, the Candidate, to "say something" to calm the people as they desperately fought for the lives of the downed politicians. Manning the podium, Redford scanned the vicious currents and whirlpools of the crazed arena. Finally, overwhelmed by the sight, he began a cynical monologue capitalizing on earlier campaign rhetoric. Pounding the podium, he yelled into the microphone in order to surface above the deafening crowd: "We're OK! There's nothing wrong with us." All the while the cameras delivered closeups of bodies crushed in the scramble, screaming women, fistfights and general hysteria as every technique was employed to save one's own skin. Although the story was political, I couldn't help but see a spiritual parallel.

WHAT SANCTUARY DO WE SEEK?

The word "sanctuary" carries two distinct meanings:

1) A holy place, a building set aside for *worship* of a god

2) A place of *refuge* or *protection; asylum*

Webster's New World Dictionary elaborates—

> Fugitives from justice were immune from arrest in churches or other sacred places—immunity from punishment or the law . . .[1]

While many clergymen today are willing to talk *about* sin or sinners they are usually hesitant to speak *at* them. The underlying thought is probably that their presence in the congregation is as much as can be hoped for, a critique made by Malcolm Muggeridge:

> One of the most effective defense systems against God's incursions has hitherto been organized religion. Various churches have provided a refuge for fugitives from God—His voice drowned in the

chanting, His smell lost in the incense, His purpose obscurred and confused in creeds, dogmas, dissertations . . . in vast cathedrals, as in little conventicles . . . one could get away from God.[2]

As long as the sinner frequents the bars and brothels he is easy to identify, but as soon as he begins to attend church services, no one dares call him a sinner! The church sanctuary has in fact become a marvelous hiding place for sinners. Knowing that the minister will not point a finger at *his* sins, the sinner finds protection. So long as we preach *about* sin rather than *at* sin, organized religion will not ultimately minister at the personal level. As C. S. Lewis has said, ". . . Corporate guilt perhaps *cannot* be, and certainly *is not*, felt with the same force as personal guilt."[3]

NEW TESTAMENT SERMONS

Personal guilt was more difficult to hide during New Testament times, primarily as a result of the emphasis of early sermons. Although the particular design of these sermons varied, the overall fabric was identical. As we look at a sampling of excerpts from four of the New Testament's most prominent preachers, note the lack of modern camouflage in their message, and the recurring theme of repentance.

PETER

Now when they heard this, they were pricked in their heart, and said unto Peter and to the rest of the apostles, Men and brethren, what shall we do? Then Peter said unto them, Repent, and be baptized every one of you in the name of Jesus Christ for the remission of sins, and ye shall receive the gift of the Holy Ghost.

Acts 2:37–38

But those things, which God before had showed by the mouth of all his prophets, that Christ should suffer, he hath so fulfilled. Repent ye therefore, and be converted, that your sins may be blotted out, when the times of refreshing shall come from the presence of the Lord.

Acts 3:18–19

JOHN THE BAPTIST

Now in those days John the Baptist came, preaching in the wilderness of Judea, saying, "Repent, for the kingdom of heaven is at hand" . . . But when he saw many of the Pharisees and Sadducees coming for baptism, he said to them, "You brood of vipers, who warned you to flee from the wrath to come? Therefore bring forth fruit in keeping with your repentance."

Matthew 3:1–2,7–8 (NASB)

PAUL

And the times of this ignorance God winked at; but now commandeth all men everywhere to repent: because he hath appointed a day, in which he will judge the world in righteousness by that man whom he hath ordained; whereof he hath given assurance unto all men, in that he hath raised him from the dead.

Acts 17:30–31

Whereupon, O king Agrippa, I was not disobedient unto the heavenly vision: But [I] showed first unto them of Damascus, and at Jerusalem, and throughout all the coasts of Judea, and then to the Gentiles, that they should repent and turn to God, and do works meet for repentance.

Acts 26:19–20

JESUS

Now after that John was put in prison, Jesus came into Galilee, preaching the gospel of the kingdom of God, and saying, The time is fulfilled, and the kingdom of God is at hand: repent ye, and believe the gospel.

Mark 1:14–15

I tell you, Nay: but, except ye repent, ye shall likewise perish.

Luke 13:5

Then began he to upbraid the cities wherein most of his mighty works were done, because they repented not: Woe unto thee Chorazin! woe unto thee Bethsaida! for if the mighty works, which were done in you, had been done in Tyre and Sidon, they would have repented long ago in sackcloth and ashes.

Matthew 11:20–21

THE PREREQUISITE

Although a great deal of attention is given to the theme of repentance by the New Testament writers, it is never mentioned as an *end* in itself. Rather, repentance is a *means* to salvation. It is what Solzhenitsyn refers to as "a clearing of the ground."[4] Repentance is the condition of, or the *prerequisite* to, salvation. Jesus makes this clear when, in Mark 1:15, He exhorts the people to repent and believe the gospel. *Repentance alone will not save you; but unless you repent you cannot be saved.*

One of the most astonishing things I have read in recent years was a Christian book on the plan of salvation which actually suggested that repentance was *subordinate* to faith. Here is the result of the Commercial Transaction Theory: salvation is totally God's responsibility—He's done everything—He's paid for your sin; therefore, just simply accept what's already been done. They come to Christ to get; to receive an *unconditional* gift. This was most certainly not the case in biblical times. This current type of teaching will never result in sinners realizing their sin and coming broken and contrite to the foot of the cross like the convicted publican.

The tax-gatherer, standing some distance away, was even unwilling to lift up his eyes to heaven, but was beating his breast, saying, 'God, be merciful to me, *the* sinner!' I tell you, this man went down to his house justified . . . He who humbles himself shall be exalted.

Luke 18:13–14 (NASB)

Here a man encountered his own sin; he didn't refer to himself merely as *a sinner* but rather as *the sinner*. The man was ashamed to even lift up his eyes. As the realization came into sharper focus, he cried out to God for mercy! The men of Jerusalem responded in similar fashion to the anointed preaching of Peter.

Now when they heard this, they were pierced to the heart, and said to Peter and the rest of the apostles, "Brethren, what shall we do?" And Peter said to them, "Repent and let each of you be baptized in the name of Jesus Christ for the forgiveness of your sins; and you shall receive the gift of the Holy Spirit."

Acts 2:37–38 (NASB)

What a rare sight! How often has modern preaching affected men to the point they were *pierced to the heart* and came *asking* how to be saved?

Our trite little formula of "just accept Jesus" has produced countless spiritual stillbirths and inoculated millions of others against the true gospel. The question, "Will you accept Jesus?" implies some doubt about His acceptability! We must remember that Christianity is, in essence, a relationship between a man and his God. *We* have broken the relationship. *We* have left God in the act of rebellion to pursue our own idea of happiness. Surely if we are going to be reconciled to God after all this, it must be on His conditions. There seems to have been an inversion of biblical injunctives. It is not whether we "accept" Christ, but whether Christ accepts us. That is the crucial issue. Will Christ indeed accept us the way we are as so many today imply? Will the King of Kings come to rule over a moral garbage dump? The notion that the sinner's condition is irrelevant at salvation shows how little we know of our responsibility in salvation, as well as God's character.

C. S. Lewis asks:

> When we fall in love with a woman, do we cease to care whether she is clean or dirty, fair or foul? . . . Does any woman regard it as a sign of love in a man that he neither knows nor cares how she is looking?[5]

The Lord Jesus refers to man's solemn responsibility in salvation with His warning to would-be disciples:

> For which one of you, when he wants to build a tower, does not first sit down and calculate the cost, to see if he has enough to complete it? Otherwise, when he has laid a foundation, and is not able to finish, all who observe it begin to ridicule him, saying, 'This man began to build and was not able to finish.'
>
> Luke 14:28–30 (NASB)

One of the greatest deterrents to the conversion of sinners today are the "half-built" Christians so evident across our land. From the very beginning they were instructed by pastors, priests and laymen that they were acceptable to God the way they were. Thus the idols which remain in their hearts (presumably to be dealt with later) bring ridicule to God's name. Where does the Bible teach that a turning from or a forsaking of *all known sin* is not an absolute essential condition of salvation? The popular theory that the sinner is "clothed with Christ's righteousness" to cover up the actual presence of ongoing sin, makes God appear as the biggest dupe in the universe! If God cannot have fellowship with unrighteousness, and we are leading unrighteous lives (except for Christ's righteousness), then we can only conclude that God's relationship is actually with Himself! The notion that God enjoys fellowship with those who are sinners by glancing at Christ's righteousness beside him is unrealistic.*

INVITATION OR COMMANDMENT?

The question of whether repentance is equal or subordinate to faith is open to interpretation. Is repentance issued as an invitation or a commandment? If repentance is an invitation, then our response is *relative*; if it is a commandment, then our response must be *absolute*. If repentance is a commandment of God, then it is ludicrous to think we can give it a subordinate status. No commandment of God is less important than another. We must keep them all. The following reasons show that repentance is a commandment and not an invitation.

1— God specifically refers to repentance as a commandment. "God . . . now commandeth all men everywhere to repent." (Acts 17:30)

2— If repentance were an invitation, there would be no punishment for those who refused. Yet Jesus said, "Except ye repent, ye shall all likewise perish" (Luke 13:3).

3— There is no passage of scripture in the entire Bible that indicates repentance is optional.

If we really believed that repentance was a commandment rather than an optional invitation, this would drastically alter the complexion of today's Church. We would recognize that those who refused to repent were just not "growing in the Lord", but were actually guilty of disobedience.

*The present day church seems to have missed the whole meaning of 2 Corinthians 5:21 because it is only a happy submission to Christ (or a right relationship) that is referred to by the phrase "in Christ" (see also Chapter 2). Anselm admitted a 'non-personal' transference of Christ's merit to men, a point which so enthusiastic a champion as Brunner thinks a fault (Gustaf Aulen, *Christus Victor* (Macmillan) p. 92).

IS THE BATTLE OVER?

Christian speaker Winkie Pratney often refers to the Japanese surrender in the Pacific at the close of World War II. The formal surrender took place aboard the battleship Missouri, between the Japanese admiral and General Douglas MacArthur, commander of the Allied Forces in the Pacific. As the highly decorated admiral, replete with all the regalia of war, offered his hand of surrender to the American general, MacArthur replied, "Your sword first please, sir."

We must also surrender our weapons of rebellion before we can hope to be reconciled to our former enemy. For as long as we cling to our selfishness, we indicate our intention of entertaining a prolonged conflict. When we acknowledge sin as willful defiance and lawless rebellion, we also acknowledge that a *surrender* rather than a *cure* is needed. "That every mouth may be stopped, and all the world may become guilty before God" (Romans 3:19).

If a love of sin remains in the heart, the sinner remains unrepentant.* The individual whose heart is full of pride is unwilling to be known openly for what he or she really is. As long as denial and deception are present, no repentance has taken place. Those who cling to their opinions, habits and possessions simply do not mean business with God. They self-righteously display a token commitment while tailoring doctrine to suit their conduct. Painstakingly they construct excuses to conceal their love for the world, apparently unaware or unconcerned about the warning of scripture:

> Do not be deceived, God is not mocked; for whatever a man sows, this he will also reap.
> Galatians 6:7 (NASB)

We must come to God with empty hands and broken hearts, for God will not play games with the religious trifler:

---

*It needs to be mentioned here that there is a difference between "a love of sin" and "temptation to sin." An individual who loves or enjoys sin has no intention of really terminating it through repentance or a new change of direction.

> Repent, and *turn* yourselves *from all* your trans-
> gressions. . . . *Cast away* from you *all* your trans-
> gressions. . . .
>
> Ezekiel 18:30–31

No attempt must be made to conceal any selfishness, for God declares in His Word that "He that covereth his sins shall not prosper" (Prov. 28:13). In keeping one you might as well keep them all; for in desiring to hold on to your sin, you indicate your intention to continue battle.

SEE—HATE—FORSAKE

True repentance involves our entire personality in a confrontation with sin. We must first see our sin through God's eyes for the abhorrent thing it is; only then will we be able to hate our sin with a righteous passion. Given our tendency to hold on to sin we love, this thorough hatred of sin must precede a genuine forsaking it.

To begin this process, one must take a long and thoughtful look, first, at what sin has done to God and, second, at His loving and merciful response to us in spite of the abuse He has suffered. The Bible tells us that it is "the *goodness* of God (that) leadeth thee to repentance" (Rom. 2:4), not *fear* or *force*. The love of God displayed on Calvary was the greatest possible force to subdue the human heart, and for those who fail to receive the knowledge, the message of scripture is solemn.

> For if we go on sinning willfully after receiving the knowledge of the truth, there no longer re-mains a sacrifice for sins, but a certain terrifying expectation of judgment, and *the fury of a fire which will consume the adversaries.*
>
> Hebrews 10:26–27 (NASB)

SEEING OUR SIN—"Repentance is always difficult; not only because we must cross the threshold of self-love, but also because our own sins are not easily visible to us."[6] However, when we release ourselves to the control of the

Holy Spirit, He releases us from our subjective shells so that we are able, perhaps for the first time, to view sin from God's objective vantage point.

Once Job had a vision of himself in relation to God's loving kindness when he declared:

> I have heard of Thee by the hearing of the ear; but now my eye sees Thee; therefore I retract, and I repent in dust and ashes.
>
> Job 42:5–6 (NASB)

From this elevated perspective we are able to see the true nature of sin and its fraudulent pleasures.

> But when Simon Peter saw that, he fell down at Jesus' feet, saying, "Depart from me, for I am a sinful man, O Lord!"
>
> Luke 5:8 (NASB)

HATING OUR SIN—While it is virtually impossible to hate our sin before we see it exposed, once we do see and recognize its diabolical qualities and truly repent, we actually do detest that for which we once held a strange fascination.

> "Yet even now," declares the Lord, "Return to Me with all your heart, and with fasting, weeping and mourning."
>
> Joel 2:12 (NASB)

During the course of his investigation into the causes of the religious superficiality in many of the churches of his day, American revivalist Charles Grandison Finney noted this characteristic of true repentance:

> The individual who truly repents, not only sees sin to be detestable and vile, and *worthy* of abhorrence, but he *really* abhors it, and hates it in his heart . . . You do not now abstain from it through fear, and to avoid punishment, but *because you hate it* . . . in relation to God, he feels towards sin as it really is. And here is the source of those gushings

> of sorrow in which Christians sometimes break
> out when contemplating sin. The Christian views
> it as to its nature, and simply feels abhorrence.
> But when he views it in relation to God, then he
> weeps.[7]

This seems indeed the sorrow which produces a genuine repentance.

> For the sorrow that is according to the will of God
> produces a repentance without regret. . . .
> 2 Corinthians 7:10 (NASB)

FORSAKING OUR SIN—As mentioned earlier, the entire personality is involved in the act of repentance. Our *minds*, enlightened through the revelation of the Holy Spirit, are able to perceive sin stripped of all pretense. *Emotionally* we respond to this understanding with considerable revulsion, pain and sorrow. But the final and crucial stage involves our *will* in the actual severance and forsaking of sin. This stage will always follow *if* repentance is genuine. If we have not truly seen our sin, or if we have seen it and yet *love* it, there is little chance that it will be forsaken.

> If iniquity is in your hand, put it far away, and do
> not let wickedness dwell in your tents.
> Job 11:14 (NASB)

> The scope of our repentance must be infinite. We
> cannot run away even from ancient sins; we may
> write off other people's sins as ancient history, but
> we have no right to do it for ourselves.[8]

Restitution in all applicable cases is an important corollary of repentance and is usually a fairly reliable indicator that a genuine repentance has occurred.[9]

DON'T BE FOOLED

As we close this chapter, noting the tendency of human

nature to take the easy way, we will look briefly at what repentance *is not*.

1) Repentance is not a *confession of sin*.

Catholic confession booths and Protestant altars have been the cathartic contact points of sinners for centuries. The problem all too often is that sin is confessed because the guilt of sin is making life uncomfortable and not because it is an offense to God. Many people attend church on Sunday morning not because they want to honor God's name, but because the lingering guilt of sin might spoil their afternoon.

Sin is often confessed complete with a fervent display of emotions, not because the sinner wants to turn from the sin which he detests, but to obtain relief from the emotional burden which accompanies it. Although God wants to hear our sincere confessions, their root cause is what He desires to eliminate. In other words, the Bible requires that we not only *confess* our sin but that we *turn* from it as well.

2) Repentance is not *remorse or contrition* over sin.

Although remorse, sorrow and contrition are involved in a repentant attitude, they do not in themselves comprise biblical repentance. Many have wept at church altars only to arise unchanged and eventually engage in the same sins over which they wept. Unfortunately, tears have such a powerful effect on most of us that our tendency is to conclude genuine repentance must have taken place. It has often been said that heaven is full of repentant sinners, while hell is full of remorseful ones.

Whenever we realize the truth about our sin and yet decide to remain unchanged, rejecting the ramifications of true repentance, great frustration results. We feel remorse and sorrow; we hate ourselves. Remaining unchanged and trapped between what we know is right and what we still wrongly love, we slowly experience the death of our personalities. This is the very opposite of the godly sorrow which "produces a repentance without regret" ultimately *freeing* us from our bondange.

Repentance, then, is an intelligent choice to renounce our selfish motives in life as we are humbled by an encounter with the cross and gently wooed and convicted by the Holy Spirit. Our entire personality is involved in a change of opinion, a change of feeling and, finally, a determined renunciation and forsaking of all known sin. This is the first and only proper step for all who have been involved in a persistent rebellion against God and His kingdom.

FAITH

7/SEEING IS BELIEVING

Salvation—Phase Two

> Christian faith . . . is the firm conviction that the self-disclosure of God in Jesus Christ is the ultimate truth of what is. It is a reasonable decision after rational reflection.
>
> Os Guiness

> Real faith is not the stuff dreams are made of; rather it is tough, practical and altogether realistic. Faith sees the invisible but it does not see the nonexistent.
>
> A.W. Tozer

> To believe truly is to will firmly.
>
> Andrew Murray

The apostle Paul speaks of "testifying to both Jews and Greeks of *repentance* toward God and *faith* in our Lord Jesus Christ" (Acts 20:21). Having previously discussed to some degree the nature and necessity of repentance, we now turn our attention to the matter of faith.

Faith today almost defies definition. To the secularist, the faith of the religious man is a rather pitiful, mindless exercise. Ambrose Bierce defined faith as, "Belief without evidence in what is told by one who speaks without knowledge of things without parallel."[1] To the religious man, faith is the truth of what really is. But even within the church the definition of faith is adrift. What is faith? Is it a set-jaw determination or an intellectual endorsement of facts? Is it a believing of the truth? (If you think *faith* is hard to define, try truth.) Or is faith a commitment, a surrendering of the will, an obedience? About the only thing unanimously agreed upon is that faith is necessary for salvation.

INTELLECTUAL FAITH AND SAVING FAITH

Faith is often used in the Bible, and almost invariably by the secular world as well, to indicate a *firm, intellectual belief* in something. Christians often assume it to mean an acceptance of the doctrines of Christianity. With this definition, we understand a series of facts or creeds accompanied by adequate evidence to assure us they are true. It is this type of faith, designated by the Greek word *pepoitha*, which means "to be persuaded."

> And when they had set a day for him, they came to him at his lodging in large numbers; and he was explaining to them by solemnly testifying about the kingdom of God, and trying to persuade them concerning Jesus, from both the Law of Moses and from the Prophets, from morning until evening. And some were being persuaded by the things spoken, but others would not believe.
>
> Acts 28:23–24 (NASB)

Although this type of faith or persuasion *leads us* to the truth, it is utterly impossible that a mere intellectual state will *save* us. It is this type of believing, for example, which James indicates even demons possess.

> Thou believest that there is one God; thou doest well: the devils also believe, and tremble.
>
> James 2:19

Christian faith encompasses an intellectual faith, but is not exactly equivalent to it. In other words, *one is not ultimately saved by believing, but one must believe in order to be saved*. As Os Guiness points out, the *will*, not merely the intellect, is involved.

> Becoming a Christian is an authentic choice of a whole man; it involves his reason, his emotions and his *will*; it is in this sense that faith is *more than rational*.[2]

Operating under the law of cause and effect, the mind and emotions are not virtuous. Virtue is part of the will; it is therefore free from the law of cause and effect. In saving faith the *heart is committed* to the mind's realization and acknowledgment of the following:

1) That we are guilty* and morally corrupt
2) That God is holy and merciful
3) That Christ came into the human situation and sacrificed his life on our behalf

Let us explore more fully the avenues of faith.

SUBSTANCE AND EVIDENCE

Now faith is the substance of things hoped for, the evidence of things not seen.

Hebrews 11:1

Faith is that principle, that exercise of mind and soul, which has for its object things not seen but hoped for, and instead of sinking under them as too ponderous, whether from their difficulty or from their uncertainty, stands firm under them— supports and sustains their pressure—in other words, is assured of, confides in and relies on them.[3]

A solid understanding of the biblical ingredients mentioned above in Hebrews will help us steer clear of the popular mystical nonsense taught today under the guise of faith.

SUBSTANCE—This declares that *something is there*, even though its form may be difficult to recognize. In the Greek language, the word for substance is *hupostasis*. This word actually consists of two words:

*Remember—repentance doesn't mean that we cease to be *guilty*—but that we cease to sin.

Hupo—under
Histemi—stand
It is that which *stands under*.

Substance is *not* the object hoped for; it is rather that which, as Dr. John W. Follette said, "stands under and supports that object in bringing it into material manifestation."[4]

> . . . for what a man seeth, why doth he yet hope for?
>
> Romans 8:24

You cannot have both faith and materialism. God does not want us to say we have the material object when we don't. This applies to the gifts of the Spirit as well as salvation, and particularly needs to be mentioned today concerning the area of physical healing. God wants us to declare our faith and say we have *hupostasis* or *assurance* that the material object hoped for will become a reality. Faith is not a struggle. We do not need to go through mental and emotional gymnastics in order to secure it. Faith is a *rest* . . . a calm assurance and a support—it stands under!

> (Abraham) staggered not at the promise of God through unbelief; but was strong in faith, giving glory to God.
>
> Romans 4:20

When we waver concerning the promise of God, it is because of *fear* and *unbelief*, when we have no solid foundation. As for real stability, we have only to consider God's character.

> Every good thing bestowed and every perfect gift is from above, coming down from the Father of lights, with whom there is *no variation*, or shifting shadow.
>
> James 1:17 (NASB)

"Faith . . . is the art of holding on to things your reason has once accepted, in spite of your changing moods."[5] This statement from C.S. Lewis reminds us that

Abraham and a host of others like him were able to stand like the rock of Gibraltar because of the *hupostasis* which supported them.

> True faith is never found alone; it is always accompanied by expectation. The man who believes the promises of God expects to see them fulfilled. Where there is no expectation there is no faith.[6]

EVIDENCE—Is there sufficient evidence, open to verifiable observation, which can offer strong arguments for believing that God is there and is who He says He is?

> . . . there must be no divorce between premises and evidences. Premises without evidences are unsupported; evidences without premises are insufficient.[7]

Many feel that because faith has to do with unseen and immaterial things, there is either no such thing as evidence or, if there is, it is irrelevant to true faith. But *faith is not believing without evidence*. A man is under no *obligation* to believe. In fact, he *cannot* believe a thing without surveying evidence. There are those who will dispute such a statement, contending that it *is* possible to believe without necessarily seeing any evidence.[8] One needs to carefully consider this argument.

To begin, what exactly do some believe without any evidence whatsoever to support that belief? *No evidence* is not *limited evidence*. Limited evidence is often spoken of as if it were the believer's final bastion. Declarations such as, "We can only trust His character," or, "I believe it because God's Word says so," are good examples of this. Certainly God's character and His word are evidences where we can solidly plant our faith. We know God's character, not because some Christian book describes it, but because He has chosen to reveal it. If God had never revealed His character to us, it would not be an evidence. The fact He has demonstrated it in nature and in lives throughout history is a cause for rejoicing. Furthermore, who really believes the

Bible "just because it says so?" This is philosophical circularity. There are many other religious books today also claiming to be repositories of truth. There are, however, several prominent distinctives which the Bible alone possesses and which set it apart from all other literature, religious or otherwise—and this is why we revere it. We believe the Bible is God's Word because we have *evidence* that it is.

Were there no existent evidence disclosing God's character and expectations, one could not possibly *know* Him, let alone *believe* Him. It this case, belief would be stupidity, not faith, for faith requires *some* evidence. The leap of faith popularized by the existentialists, notably Sören Kierkegaard, is the desperate attempt to find meaning . . . or in the religious sense, God, by a chance plunge into the unknown. What then is the difference between Christian faith and existentialism? *Evidence.* The existentialist hopes to find reality in a mindless "leap of faith," while the Christian knows what awaits him *before* he steps onto the road where he "walks by faith and not by sight." Dr. Francis Schaeffer illustrates this concept very well:

> The scene is a guided, alpine expedition caught high on the bare rock by a sudden, dense fog. The guide turns to the party and tells them ice is forming and before morning they will all freeze to death on the mountain. About an hour or so later, as the situation progressively worsens, a member of the party says to the guide: "Suppose I were to drop and hit a ledge ten feet down in the fog. What would happen then?" The guide replies that he might survive until morning and thus live. The individual then, without any warning, hangs and drops into the fog. This is the existential leap of faith.

> Supposing, on the other hand, we hear a voice calling out to us as we cling to our precarious positions. The voice says, "You can't see me, but I know exactly where you are from your voices. I am on another ridge. I've lived in these mountains for over sixty years and I know every foot of them. I assure you there is a ledge ten feet below

you and if you'll drop to it, you can make
it through the night and I'll get you in the
morning."[9]

After asking a series of pertinent questions and receiving
convincing answers, you would no doubt drop. Here is faith
in the true sense—faith with evidence.

Substance and evidence are further revealed in the account of Peter's abortive attempt to walk on the Sea of Galilee.

> And immediately He made the disciples get into
> the boat, and go ahead of Him to the other side,
> while He sent the multitudes away. And after He
> had sent the multitudes away, He went up to the
> mountain by Himself to pray; and when it was
> evening, He was there alone. But the boat was al-
> ready many stadia away from the land, battered
> by the waves; for the wind was contrary. And in
> the fourth watch of the night He came to them,
> walking upon the sea. And when the disciples
> saw Him walking on the sea, they were
> frightened, saying "It is a ghost!" And they cried
> out for fear. But immediately Jesus spoke to them,
> saying "Take courage, it is I; do not be afraid."
> And Peter answered Him and said, "Lord, if it is
> You, command me to come to You on the water."
> And He said, "Come!" And Peter got out of the
> boat, and walked on the water and came toward
> Jesus. But seeing the wind, he became afraid, and
> beginning to sink, he cried out, saying, "Lord,
> save me!" And immediately Jesus stretched out
> His hand and took hold of him, and said to him,
> "O you of little faith, why did you doubt?"
>
> Matthew 14:22–31 (NASB)

Where did Peter find the faith to venture into a situation so
totally beyond his own abilities? If the object of Peter's faith
was *not* beyond himself then faith would have been totally
unnecessary here.

The miracle begins as Peter receives evidence—Jesus
bids him *come*. The powerful assurance and conviction
within his heart subsquent to the divine "come" was the

156

substance *(hupostasis)* that brought forth the miracle. Jesus' rebuke, "O thou of little faith, wherefore didst thou doubt?," doesn't refer to Peter's honest skepticism prior to any evidence, but to his failure to persevere *after* he had received a word from the Lord. Many Christians venture out on a promise when it has no application to the situation at all. Great confusion and damage may occur because of our presumption. We would be well warned to never venture out upon the water without a divine *"come"* under our feet!

FAITH AS COMMITMENT

Having discussed the intellectual faith which leads us to salvation, we now turn our attention to saving faith. Intellectual faith is a matter of *mental deduction,* whereas saving faith concerns *volitional action.* This is why saving faith is represented as a virtue in the Bible. *A man is not saved simply because he comes to a mental deduction of some sort.* There is no indication whatsoever in the scriptures that a man can simply acknowledge or believe something and get to heaven. Saving faith, as we shall see, has more to it than that.

Interestingly enough, the word which is often rendered *faith* in the New Testament *(pistis)* is also rendered *commit.* Saving faith is represented in the scriptures as a full committal of will to the fact that a holy God sent His Son Jesus to earth where He willingly sacrificed His life so that we might receive forgiveness of all past sin and guilt. It is a full recognition that in all the boundless reaches of the universe there is no other solution to our desperate situation.

We have probably all seen the little buttons some Christians are currently wearing on their pockets with the glib inscription, "Try Jesus." The idea conveyed to the unsaved passerby is that if he will just poke his head into Christianity, he will be positively enchanted with Christ and ultimately want to believe in Him. This solicitation to "try before you buy," as if salvation were a commodity to be tossed experimentally in one's spiritual shopping cart, is absolutely inadequate. It's not so much the fact that people have put out an advertisement for God that is disturbing, although in the end this sort of nonsensical behavior will undoubtedly be revealed for the trite foolishness it is, but the idea that Jesus can be "tried" contains hellish deception. An individual isn't saved by "Trying Jesus", but by being "thoroughly persuaded" and then *acting* upon the data. The Bible teaches that salvation is a matter of: 1) obedience, 2) commitment, and 3) slavery. It is impossible to give a piece of your heart to God on a trial basis.

> Do you not know that when you present your-selves to someone as slaves for obedience, you are slaves of the one whom you obey, either of sin resulting in death, or of obedience resulting in righteousness? But thanks be to God that though you were slaves of sin, you became obedient from the heart to that form of teaching to which you were committed, and having been freed from sin, you became slaves of righteousness.
>
> Romans 6:16–18 (NASB)

It is highly unlikely that one can come to Jesus without being enslaved to Him. "Christianity is preeminently the religion of slaves," Simone Weil once said. "Slaves cannot help belonging to it."[10] The death of Christ shatters the hold of sin on our lives and frees us to become love slaves. The whole process is, in effect, a "changing of masters."

> And He died for all, that they who live should no longer live for themselves, but for Him who died and rose again on their behalf.
>
> 2 Corinthians 5:15 (NASB)

Those initiated to Christ on a trial basis become yo-yo Christians who fling themselves on God in apparent committal, but the reins of whose lives are carefully wrapped around their fingers so when the heat is on they can quickly recall their "commitment." This is the very antithesis of biblical commitment. The New Testament word *pistis* mentioned earlier means "to trust or confide in", while the Hebrew equivalent *gagal* means "to roll". How suggestive this word is! There is no room for yo-yo commitment in this definition, for *everything* leaves the hand. What has left your hands is no longer under your control—everything belongs to Him.

> Or do you not know that your body is a temple of the Holy Spirit who is in you, whom you have from God, and that *you are not your own?* For you have been bought with a price: therefore glorify God in your body.
>
> 1 Corinthians 6:19–20 (NASB)

Paul reminds us of the costly grace which was later to be so eloquently explained by German theologian Dietrich Bonhoeffer:

> Such grace is *costly* because it calls us to follow, and it is grace because it calls us to follow Jesus Christ. It is costly because it costs a man his life, and it is grace because it gives a man the only true life. It is costly because it condemns sin, and grace because it justifies the sinner. Above all, it is costly because it cost God the life of His Son: 'Ye were bought at a price,' and what has cost God much cannot be cheap for us. Above all, it is grace because God did not reckon His Son too dear a price to pay for our life . . . costly grace is the incarnation of God.[11]

The man or woman who comes to Christ in saving faith must be absolutely convinced that the sufferings of Jesus were accomplished for them as the only remedy for their sin. The Holy Spirit will then lay open the cross of Jesus explicitly to our minds, until the revelation of our sin and God's love breaks down our will that it may be yielded completely. It is this giving of our will, this commitment of heart, which constitutes saving faith.

Faith is not embracing what one *doesn't* understand—that is magic. Saving faith is a willful embrace of what *is* understood. It must be said, however, that saving faith is a *joint effort* between man and the Holy Spirit. When one is willing to believe, the Spirit of God will give the *ability* to believe.

THE FAITH VS. WORKS CONTROVERSY

In every discussion of theology, the potential exists for endless debate on the strengths and finer points of one particular view over another. Many who allow themselves to become enmeshed in these sorts of debates often lose their perspective. Often *tradition* is unwittingly placed on a par with *truth*. Words and ideas originally intended to inspire a spiritual revolution in men's hearts are converted into a *system* for rationalizing and defending a status quo. Theology which was once vibrant because it related everything to *relationship* with God has nearly vanished. Today theology doesn't necessarily apply to our relationship; it can be *technical* without being *experiential*. With a bottling up of life into religious bureaucracy, doctrine is converted into dogma—and eventually the function of doctrine becomes less that of guidance, as far as conduct within a relationship, and more a *justification* of things as they are, or as the contemporary Sanhedrin wishes to make them.

Before we proceed, let us define what is known as *antinomianism*. The Antinomian believes that faith alone, without obedience to moral law, is all that is necessary for salvation. One might say the Antinomian's favorite hymn is "Only Believe." The Antinomian is inclined to stress the fact that man plays no part whatsoever in salvation. Repentance and the lordship of Christ are considered subtle forms of works in which man might take pride.

In light of our discussion concerning the appliction of all theology to our individual relationship with Christ, antinomianism does not fit. There cannot be a relationship unless there is a minimum of *two responsive parties*. Although the Bible clearly teaches that it is God providing and initiating salvation, man must *respond* to these overtures. If he does not, *no relationship exists*.

To equate man's responses to God's gift of salvation with the works of the flesh mentioned by the apostle Paul is utterly without foundation. If it were true that God repented for us, He would of necessity be repenting to Himself. How much easier it is to see that man, the rebel, humbled by God's goodness, chooses to cast down his weapons of warfare and engage in a logical relationship meaningful to both parties. How one could possibly take pride in truly repenting is inconceivable. Obedience to Jesus Christ as the Lord of our lives is commanded throughout Scripture. This could not possibly be considered a subtle form of works; on the contrary, this is indeed salvation!

> And when he had called the people unto him with his disciples also, he said unto them, 'Whosoever will come after me, let him deny himself, and take up his cross and follow me. For whosoever will save his life shall lose it; but whosoever shall lose his life for my sake and the gospel's, the same shall save it.'
>
> Mark 8:34–35

Note that in this scripture Jesus does not state that a man should deny himself *things*; yet it is precisely this type of denial which we find so prevalent in the church today. We deny ourselves thirty minutes each night before bed for Bible reading and ten percent of each paycheck in the offering plate. We then think in so doing we have pleased God. Concentration on denying ourselves things *is* a form of works. The Pharisees practiced great self-denial in all areas—except their hearts! This form of denial has never been acceptable to God. The words are clear enough, "let him deny *himself.*"

In the book of James we find a passage which antinomian thinkers are forever attempting to explain away. James discusses the relationship of faith and works, applying it very logically and naturally to the God-man relationship:

> What use is it, my brethren, if a man says he has faith, but he has no works? Can that faith save him? If a brother or sister is without clothing and in need of daily food, and one of you says to them, 'Go in peace, be warmed and be filled'; and yet you do not give them what is necessary for their body; what use is that? Even so faith, if it has no works, is dead, being by itself. But someone may well say, 'You have faith, and I have

works; show me your faith without works, and I will show you my faith by my works.' You believe that God is one. You do well; the demons also believe, and shudder. But are you willing to recognize, you foolish fellow, that faith without works is useless? Was not Abraham our father justified by works, when he offered up Issac his son on the altar? You see that faith was working with his works, and as a result of the works, faith was perfected; and the Scripture was fulfilled which says, 'And Abraham believed God, and it was reckoned to him as righteousness,' and he was called the friend of God. You see that a man is justified by works, and not by faith alone. And in the same way was not Rahab the harlot also justified by works, when she received the messengers and sent them out by another way? For just as the body without the spirit is dead, so also faith without works is dead.

James 2:14–16 (NASB)

A thoughtful reading of this passage provides the following striking conclusions:

1) *"Just believing"* won't save anyone. James mentions the man who says he has faith but displays no godly works and then asks the rhetorical question, "Can that faith save him"?

2) *A mental deduction is not a committal of the will with conduct to prove it.* James imagines a situation and wonders how "faith" without works would be demonstrated. He goes on to say that even demons possess this type of intellectual faith, and then implores us to forsake our foolishness and recognize that saving faith is a lifestyle, not a mystical believing.

3) *God is reasonable and sensitive, not a calculating technician.* James reminds us of the deeds in which Abraham and Rahab engaged demonstrating hearts committed to truth. When Abraham obeyed God, "he was called the friend of God."

Saving faith will produce *works of faith* (a godly lifestyle), whereas intellectual faith alone will produce *works of the flesh* (dead rituals).

By the way, I bought a fourteen-foot boat last week. I have named the two oars, one faith, the other works. I have found that if I row ever so hard with faith alone, I go round and round in a circle; and strange as it seems, works does the same thing—gets me nowhere. But when I bend my back and pull both faith and works, I can get to where I want to go.

Dr. George Winters

SAVED BY FAITH OR GRACE?

For by grace you have been saved through faith; and that not of yourselves; it is a gift of God; not as a result of works, that no one should boast.

Ephesians 2:8–9 (NASB)

Paul brings to our attention an important point in this passage concerning the workings of salvation. Grace is mentioned as the reason *why* we are saved, while faith is mentioned as the *means* to salvation, or *how* we are saved. The emphasis here is on grace rather than faith, as well it should be. We are saved by God's grace. If it weren't for that costly grace, our faith or lack of it would be irrelevant. Grace actually means "getting something we don't deserve." When this is understood, pride will be no part of our willing response to God's free gift.

CONTINUANCE

8/KEEP THE FAITH

Salvation—Phase Three

God is easy to please, but hard to satisfy.

George MacDonald

Then said Jesus to those Jews which believed on him, If ye continue in my word, then are ye my disciples indeed.

John 8:31

An abstract Christology, a doctrinal system, a general religious knowledge on the subject of grace or on the forgiveness of sins, render discipleship superfluous . . . with an abstract idea it is possible to enter into a relation of formal knowledge, to become enthusiastic about it, and perhaps even to put it into practice; but it can never be followed in personal obedience. Christianity without the living Christ is inevitably Christianity without discipleship, and Christianity without discipleship is always Christianity without Christ. It remains an abstract idea, a myth . . . in such a religion there is trust in God, but no following of Christ.

Dietrich Bonhoeffer

While there are few who claim religion apart from an actual relationship with God, it is our purpose to prove that an abstract Christianity is the inevitable result of a faith based on abstract technicalities. We must also realize that the Christian relationship must be *continued in* to remain a relationship. As it was prior to salvation when we were alienated from God, so it is when the God-man relationship is not maintained and cultivated. Once again there is only *one willing party* and one party has never made a relationship.

WHAT IS A RELATIONSHIP?

The relationship between God and man must be first, *good* and, second, *personal*. It is possible to have a relationship that is not personal, such as that of a citizen to a governor or President, and it is certainly true that some relationships, though personal, are not good. But any good, personal relationship is made up of the following three distinct, but equally essential aspects.

INITIAL DISCOVERY—There must come a time when, through some type of revelation, we discover in a person that of which we were previously unaware; when we notice qualities in their lives that attract us to them and set them apart from others.

Lovers can often pinpoint the precise moment when they begin to notice their beloved. The realization may have come as a result of an act of unselfishness on the part of their beloved, or perhaps a banner performance under pressure. Often the realization will not come during or even immediately following the incident, but days, weeks or months afterward. In time the accumulated weight of repeated demonstrations of character slowly forces the fact out of the subconscious into conscious realization. This is the moment of initial discovery.

Although in an altogether different context, this initial discovery is also present in the love relationship between parent and child. At first, the relationship is little more than self-love on the part of the infant. The new life is a part of the parents. Their life has been transferred and extended through that of the child. In a very real sense they love the child as themselves because that child *is part* of them. Later on, however, when the child manifests his own character and personality, there is room for additional discovery.

Scripture indicates that God relates to us in virtually all potential relationships:

FRIEND

Greater love has no one than this, that one lay down his life for his friends. You are my *friends*, if you do what I command you. No longer do I call you slaves; for the slave does not know what his master is doing; but I have called you *friends*, for all things that I have heard from My Father I have made known to you.

John 15:13–15

LOVER

O my dove, in the clefts of the rock, in the secret place of the steep pathway, let me see your form, let me hear your voice; for your voice is sweet, and your form is lovely. . . . *My beloved* is mine, and I am his; He pastures his flock among the lilies.

Song of Solomon 2:14,16 (NASB)

Let us rejoice and be glad and give glory to Him, for the marriage of the Lamb has come and *His bride* has made herself ready. And it was given to her to clothe herself in fine linen, bright and clean; for the fine linen is the righteous acts of the saints.

Revelation 19:7–8 (NASB)

FAMILY

Therefore, come out from their midst and be separate, says the Lord. And do not touch what is unclean; and I will welcome you. And I will be *a father* to you, and you shall be sons and daughters to Me, says the Lord God Almighty.

2 Corinthians 6:17–18 (NASB)

MUTUAL COMMITMENT—Initial discovery can be a wonderful experience, but it will prove little more if it is not used as a stepping stone to commitment. Commitment must be on a reciprocal basis before a relationship exists. If initiative is important, response is vital. As long as one party is unwilling to commit to the other, no relationship can possibly exist.

In a proper love relationship, it is impossible for one party to be the subject while the other remains strictly the object. A relationship is an interchange; both parties are alternately both a subject and an object. Each party has a role to play whether it be initiative or response. But it must be one or the other.

DURATION—No true relationship is static; it is a dynamic phenomenon. It *moves*, it goes somewhere. A relationship will either grow or deteriorate depending on the freewill decisions of the partners. Original commitments are not necessarily lasting ones. They must be *maintained*. Commitment must move along with the relationship, for if it does not, the relationship, like a car without fuel, will come to a halt. But although a motionless car remains a car, a motionless relationship is *no relationship*. *Without commitment a relationship halts, and when a relationship halts, it ceases to exist.*

ONCE SAVED, ALWAYS SAVED?

This question is of course the primary question of the doctrine of eternal security. Adherents of this doctrine insist that an initial commitment to Christ is a binding, eternal matter. Continual commitment of faith in order to maintain a dynamic (moving) relationship is unnecessary.

> It is taught in Ephesians 1:13–14 that, after a person has believed (a finished act), he is sealed with the Holy Spirit until the redemption of the purchased possession. This passage once and for all rules out the argument that one must continue to believe. There is no need for continuous faith on the part of the saved person . . .[1]

The emphasis on an initial, rather than a continuing commitment, is clear.

We have previously mentioned that a true relationship must be maintained through the mutual consent of those involved. Eternal security advocates are quick to point out that we are talking about *salvation* and not *relationship.* Again we find a technical theology apart from an involvement theology. It is a twisted conception of relationship that leads a man to say, "He lost his *fellowship* with his Lord, but not his *salvation." Our salvation is that we are reconciled to God in a loving, happy fellowship!*

It is our responsibility to discover God's conditions in the matter of salvation, and then fulfill them! Having examined faith and repentance, we now turn our attention to the third and final condition of salvation—*continuance.*

THE "IF" CONDITION

Gordon C. Olson, in his manual entitled *Sharing Your Faith,* gives one of the finest and most concise definitions of truth, as follows:

> Truth is simply a true perspective, or a true picture in all proper proportions, of what exists.[2]

Despite many volumes written supporting a "once-saved, always-saved" doctrine, when we honestly examine the words of Scripture, we must not take the position of unqualified eternal security without question. An examination of biblical texts pins this false assurance to the floor. Continual commitment as a condition of salvation is well established. Guy Duty, in *If Ye Continue,* states:

> An impartial truth-seeker accepts facts as he finds them. He has no personal preference. A Bible doctrine cannot be established merely by someone making a dogmatic statement.[3]

Consider God's "If" condition in first the Old and then the New Testaments.

The Old Testament

But if your heart turns away and you will not obey, but are *drawn away* and worship other gods and serve them, I declare to you today that *you shall surely perish*. You shall not prolong your days in the land where you are crossing the Jordan to enter and possess it.

Deuteronomy 30:17–18 (NASB)

If you forsake the Lord and serve foreign gods, then He will turn and *do you harm and consume you after He has done good to you*.

Joshua 24:20 (NASB)

If you will fear the Lord and serve Him, and listen to His voice and not rebel against the command of the Lord, then both you and also the king who reigns over you will follow the Lord your God. And if you will not listen to the voice of the Lord, but rebel against the command of the Lord, then *the hand of the Lord will be against you. . . .*

1 Samuel 12:14–15 (NASB)

As for you, my son Solomon, know the God of your father, and serve Him with a whole heart and a willing mind; for the Lord searches all hearts, and understands every intent of the thoughts. *If* you see Him, He will let you find Him; but *if* you forsake Him, *He will reject you forever*.

1 Chronicles 28:9 (NASB)

Thus says the Lord of hosts, '*If* you will walk in My ways, and *if* you perform My service, then you will also govern My house . . . . and I will grant you free access among these who are standing here.'

Zechariah 3:7 (NASB)

The New Testament

Then Jesus said to His disciples, 'If any one wishes to come after Me, let him deny himself, and take up his cross, and follow Me.'

Matthew 16:24 (NASB)

Jesus therefore was saying to those Jews who had believed Him, "If you abide in My word, then you are truly disciples of Mine."

John 8:31 (NASB)

If you keep My commandments, you will abide in My love; just as I have kept My Father's commandments, and abide in His love.

John 15:10 (NASB)

But I buffet my body and make it my slave, lest possibly, after I have preached to others, I myself should be disqualified.

1 Corinthians 9:27 (NASB)

And although you were formerly alienated and hostile in mind, engaged in evil deeds, yet He has now reconciled you in His fleshly body through death, in order to present you before Him holy and blameless and beyond reproach—if indeed you continue in the faith firmly established and steadfast, and not moved away from the hope of the gospel that you have heard, which was proclaimed in all creation under heaven, and of which I, Paul, was made a minister.

Colossians 1:21–23 (NASB)

Pay close attention to yourself and to your teaching; persevere in these things; for as you do this you will insure salvation both for yourself and for those who hear you.

1 Timothy 4:16 (NASB)

But Christ was faithful as a Son over His house whose house we are, if we hold fast our confidence and the boast of our hope firm until the end. Therefore, just as the Holy Spirit says, "Today if you hear His voice, do not harden your hearts as when they provoked Me, as in the day of trial in the wilderness, where your fathers tried Me by testing Me, and saw My works for forty years. Therefore, I was angry with this generation, and said, "They always go astray in their heart; and they did not know My ways"; As I swore in My wrath, "They shall not enter My rest."' Take care, brethren, lest there should be in any one of you an evil unbelieving heart, in *falling away* from the living God. But encourage one another day after day, as long as it is still called 'Today,' lest any one of you be hardened by the deceitfulness of sin. For we have become partakers of Christ, *if we hold fast the beginning of our assurance firm until the end.*

Hebrews 3:6–14 (NASB)

"For in the case of *those who have once been enlightened* and have tasted of the heavenly gift and have been made partakers of the Holy Spirit, and have tasted the good word of God and the powers of the age to come, and *then have fallen away, it is impossible to renew them again to repentance*, since they again crucify to themselves the Son of God, and put Him to open shame. For ground that drinks the rain which often falls upon it and brings forth vegetation useful to those for whose sake it is tilled, receives a blessing from God; but if it yields thorns and thistles, it is worthless and close to being cursed, and it ends up being burned."

Hebrews 6:4–8 (NASB)

But My righteous one shall live by faith; and if he shrinks back, My soul has no pleasure in him. But we are not of those who *shrink back to destruction*, but of those who have faith to the preserving of the soul.

Hebrews 10:38–39 (NASB)

But one who looks intently at the perfect law, the law of liberty, and *abides by it*, not having become a forgetful hearer but an effectual doer, this man shall be blessed in what he does.

James 1:25 (NASB)

Therefore, brethren, be all the more diligent to make certain about His calling and choosing you; for as long as you *practice* these things, you will never *stumble*.

2 Peter 1:10 (NASB)

You therefore, beloved, knowing this beforehand, be on your guard lest, being carried away by the error of unprincipled men, *you fall* from your own steadfastness.

2 Peter 3:17 (NASB)

And by this we know that we have come to know Him, *if we keep* His commandments. The one who says, 'I have come to know Him,' and does not keep His commandments, is a liar, and the truth is not in him; but *whoever keeps His word*, in him the love of God has truly been perfected. By this we know that we are in Him.

1 John 2:3–5 (NASB)

As for you, let that abide in you which you heard from the beginning. *If* what you heard from the beginning *abides* in you you also will abide in the Son and in the Father.

1 John 2:24 (NASB)

For if God did not spare the natural branches, neither will He spare you. Behold then the kindness and severity of God; to those who fell, severity, but to you, God's kindness, *if you continue* in His kindness; *otherwise you also will be cut off*. And they also, if they do not continue in their unbelief, will be grafted in; for God is able to graft them in again. For if you were cut off from what is by nature a wild olive tree, how much more shall these

> who are the natural branches be grafted into their
> own olive tree?
>
> Romans 11:21–24 (NASB)

The specified if-condition lies deep in Paul's thinking. The Jews would be grafted in again 'if they abide not still in unbelief.' And the Gentiles would also be broken off 'if' they did not 'continue' in faith.[4] Jesus said:

> If a man abide not in me, he is cast forth as a branch, and is withered . . . and they are burned.
>
> John 15:6

> Here in Romans 11, Paul gave the if-condition its full force . . . There is salvation in God's covenant tree for those who 'abide' in it. Paul had no doctrine such as 'once in the Tree, always in the Tree.'[5]

God's gift of salvation can certainly never be earned nor merited. We are saved as a result of God's decision to offer us something we didn't deserve: grace. This fact however does not negate the biblical insistence that salvation is also conditional. *No condition will save us.* Fulfilling a condition merely prepares the way for God to exercise that loving grace without which we would have perished. The conditions of salvation, repentance, faith and continuance are important because God has emphasized them. Yet, as we observe God's desire to restore and then sustain a relationship with His creation, the logic behind His conditions is unmistakable.

THE SOURCE OF CONDEMNATION

Subjects such as continuance in faith, discipleship and the lordship of Jesus are shunned today by a great number of ministers as well as laypeople. But when Jesus came into our world He brought two equally significant messages:

1) His love carried no condemnation

> For God sent not His son into the world to condemn the world; but that the world through Him might be saved.
>
> John 3:17

2) His love did carry expectations

> If you love Me, you will keep My commandments. . . . He who has My commandments, and keeps them, he it is who loves Me. . . .
>
> John 14:15,21 (NASB)

The Bible tells us that Jesus did not come to condemn the world but to *save* it—to save it from those very things that were condemning it. He came to shed light in the darkness so that men, with His assistance, could view their deeds objectively. Shedding light is both a wonderful and a dangerous activity. It is wonderful for the truth seeker because he will gravitate toward the light; it is dangerous because the lover of darkness will seek to put it out.

> And this is the judgment, that the light is come into the world, and men loved the darkness rather than the light; for their deeds were evil. For everyone who does evil hates the light, and does not come to the light, lest his deeds should be exposed. But he who practices the truth comes to the light, that his deeds may be manifested as having been wrought in God.
>
> John 3:19–21 (NASB)

In Jesus' mission to redeem humankind, His ultimate aim was to win us back into relationship. He called all to follow Him, wanting us to emulate who it was we followed. He desired to be with the ones He loved, but this fellowship was to be a divine school as well.

> If any one serve Me, let him follow Me; and
> where I am, there shall My servant also be. . . .
>
> John 12:26 (NASB)

Although Jesus' love was not condemning, it was nevertheless full of expectation. When the Lord stated, "*If you love me . . . keep my commandments,*" the implication was clear that love required obedience. Jesus, knowing that we need Him, requires our total allegiance for *our sakes.* When we do not obey fully, *conviction* sets in as God lovingly prods us to keep us from damaging ourselves.

Today churches are filled with people harboring unconfessed sin in their lives. God's normal response to these who most often know better, is to send conviction. This conviction is often intensified as we are confronted through a sermon or the reproof of a friend. *If* we love our sin more than God, we will attack His servants and their message. Trying to pry the conviction out of our lives, we condemn it and blame "harsh teaching". Many who suffer from guilt feelings are suffering not from condemnation but because they *are actually guilty!* If we try to rid ourselves of that guilt which is the result of our sin through any means other than God's prescribed method of confession and repentance, we open ourselves to danger and deception. "Whoso covereth his sin shall not prosper" (Prov. 28:13).

The source, then, of condemnation is located in one of the following situations:

1) Human or demonic agents refusing to grant rest to a soul who has genuinely confessed and repented of his sin.

2) Confounding conviction and condemnation in order to soothe guilt feelings accompanying *unconfessed* sin.

The honest disciple of Christ need not experience guilt feelings if he has done in earnest all our Lord has commanded us to do.

ALTAR RELATIONSHIPS

An altar is a place of beginnings. In marriage it is the initiation of a lifelong relationship. In salvation it is the initiation of an eternal relationship.* Marriage vows are repeated in the aura of love. It is the love that gives the vows their power. Although we would like to say the vows should be a permanent, once-and-for-all exercise, for many they are not. In the United States today, we are faced with the tragic spectre of one out of every two marriages ending in divorce.

When you repeat your marriage vows, they are a public declaration of your intention to *continue* in the marriage. Without continuance, the altar and the vows are meaningless. When you prayed the "sinner's prayer", when you "confessed with your mouth", it was a public declaration of your intention to continue in faith. Here again, although we'd like to say faith is a finished act, the Bible teaches that it is possible for an individual to wander away from his first love. When the flame of love begins to flicker and we grow lukewarm, the relationship is over (Revelation 3:15–16).

Inevitably someone will propose that it is possible to be separated and out of relationship and still be legally married. We need to remember that God will not force anything on us (including His name) that we do not want. To discuss *requirements* apart from *relationship* is *legalism*. To be legally united without a relationship is legalism. A relationship must move; it cannot be left at the altar!

DISCIPLESHIP: LEGALISM OR LOVE?

Those who consider all the talk about discipleship and continuance to be a legalistic manifestation of works gener-

---

*Although the church altar in some churches is often the place where sinners make their peace with God, I am in no way inferring that it is the *only* place. Location is clearly irrelevant.

ally maintain that we ought to rest in faith alone. Whatever happens in our lives must be God's doing. It is His power working in us and through us. Although this assertion is *true*, it also stands *incomplete*. Again we must remember that when we enter into salvation, we enter a relationship. We cannot always be looking at what God will do for us. Certainly we ought to consider God's feelings in this relationship. Does He not deserve the moments of pleasure and gratification that our obedience and surrender can bring Him? Why are we always looking for theological loopholes to escape the responsibilities of a relationship?

Often the analogy is used of a child using his father's money to purchase a special gift for the father. Although the gift was purchased by means provided by the father, this does not, we are told, in any way diminish the impact of the expression. While this argument is accurate as far as it goes, it does not take into account our relationship to Christ as lover. He is spoken of as the Bridegroom, we as his bride. Don't we sing choruses to him as the "Lover of My Soul"? In this love relationship, pleasure can in no way be self-induced. It must come as a free will origination of another moral being. Only then will the soul rest in satisfaction. The rest of faith must not be considered as a *cessation of activity*, but rather an internal confidence in the character of our Beloved. As in marriage, from the altar and beyond, we relax in the surety that *we have chosen the right one.*

Discipleship is merely a "following out of love." It is to obey Christ's commandments because they are wise, loving, and for the good of our relationship. But when Jesus asks us to do something, we must learn to do *it*—rather than change the request to mean what suits *us*. Dietrich Bonhoeffer looks at this issue in light of Jesus' confrontation with the rich young man.

> We are excusing ourselves from single-minded obedience to the word of Jesus on the pretext of legalism and a supposed preference for an obedience 'in faith.' The difference between ourselves and the rich young man is that he was not al-

lowed to solace his regrets by saying: 'Never mind what Jesus says, I can still hold on to my riches . . . despite my inadequacy I can take comfort in the thought that God has forgiven me my sins and can have fellowship with Christ in faith.' But no, he went away sorrowful. Because he would not obey, he could not believe.

If Jesus said to someone: 'Leave all else behind and follow me' . . . if Jesus challenged us with the command: 'Get out of it,' we should take Him to mean: 'Stay where you are, but cultivate that inward detachment.' When orders are issued in other spheres of life there is no doubt whatsoever of their meaning. Are we to treat the commandment of Jesus differently from other orders and exchange obedience for downright disobedience? Struggling against the 'legalism' of simple obedience . . . we land ourselves in the worst kind of legalism. The only way to overcome this legalism is by real obedience to Christ when He calls us . . . by eliminating simple obedience . . . we take it for granted as we open the Bible that we have a key to its interpretation. But then the key we use would not be the Living Christ . . . the key we use is a general doctrine of grace which we can apply as we will.[6]

SPIRITUAL ASSASSINS

No one who falls away from God does so on a moment's impulse. The implications are far too severe and the hold of God is strong. There must be a plot, a plan, a conspiracy if you will, to subvert the rightful rulership of Christ in our hearts. This conspiracy unfolds over a duration of time that may even take years. But when one thinks he has gotten away with little, he will often take much. After a gradual erosion of our conscience's influence, we become ultimately open for a more full-scale revolt.

> Because the sentence against an evil deed is not
> executed quickly, therefore the hearts of the sons
> of men among them are given fully to do evil.
>
> Ecclesiastes 8:11 (NASB)

This conspiracy unfolds in the human heart. No kingdom is a bonafide kingdom unless it has a king. For every man and woman, that king will either be *King Jesus* or *King Self*. Since we are now discussing a process occurring within the Christian life, we will place the rightful ruler, King Jesus, on the throne. The conspiracy to remove Him from the heart escalates through four distinct stages.

INITIAL SIN—Usually an underground army trying to overthrow a government is comparatively small in terms of men and weapons. A hit-and-run-type warfare is often employed as an alternative to brute force. Often in situations such as the ones we have viewed recently in Zimbabwe-Rhodesia and El Salvador, warfare unfolds with a sniper's bullet downing a border guard at some remote station. Although it is highly probable that the majority of citizens in the capital city many miles away know nothing of the events, the security of the kingdom has suffered an *undetected breakdown*. If this situation is not immediately rectified by reinforcements, enemy troops will pour through the unguarded border point. It is just so in Christian life; unconfessed sin inevitably leads to the dangerous second stage of the campaign.

PERSISTENT SIN—Perhaps while still at the sniping stage, even the aggressors have no serious plans to actually assassinate the ruler. However, if the progress should continue relatively unchecked, the rebel activities will persist as *intentional plotting* begins. Killing is no longer *indiscriminate* as key members of the government are now targeted. *Honesty* is often one of the first things to go. In spite of success, we are still experiencing great pressure from our conscience, which is always pointing out our error and pleading with us to cease our activities. So we decide to move to stage three.

CONSCIENCE IS GAGGED—With the conscience bound and gagged, it makes it so much easier "to do what we have to do." The amazing thing is that nobody yet suspects our intentions, well—almost. We're still attending church and giving our ten percent. Everything has proceeded thus far with guarded caution. Yet because we are still feigning allegiance to Christ's authority, we must of necessity occasionally pass through the throne room. Oh, how His stare burns! Although we have fooled everyone else, somehow we know that He *knows*. So, we attempt to avoid Him. We do so much in the same way a man contemplating adultery avoids his wife. Whenever one avoids prayer, avoids talking to God, he is in perilous danger! But gagging the conscience will be our *last, silent maneuver.*

TOTAL DEFECT—Jesus Christ does not force His way into our lives. He is not glued to the throne of our hearts. He sits in authority only as long as we desire to be subject to Him.

He hears us stealing up behind Him, and He understands the sound of a safety being clicked off, but He will not move. He will not summon the palace guard, nor will He struggle. He will only rule as long as you want Him. Finally, the loaded revolver is placed at the base of His skull and the trigger is pulled. You have become a spiritual assassin.

Do you think one can just walk away from God at the drop of a hat? Those who suddenly and brazenly begin to mock God's people and leave the Church, belittling Christianity, have had no sudden change of heart. Their hostility had been silently brewing in their hearts for a long time. How many are there *right now* involved in one of the latter stages of this evil plot? Can we muster enough courage and spiritual sensitivity to minister to a brother whose heart is growing cold?

Karl Menninger quotes one pastor sick over the spiritual frigidity of his parishioners:

> Here they come,
> my nonchalants,
> my lazy daisies,
> their dainty perfume
> disturbing the room

the succulent smell
seductive as hell.

Here they are
my pampered flamboyants,
status spoiled, who bring
with exquisite zing
their souls spick and span
protected by Ban,

their hearts young and gay
decked in handsome cliché,
exchanging at my call
with no effort at all
worship for whispering
God for gossiping,
theology for television.

Baptized in the smell
of classic Chanel
I promote their nod
to a jaunty God
Who, they are sure,
is a sparkling gem
superbly right for them.

There they go
my in-crowd
my soft-skinned crowd,
my suntanned, so-so
elegant, swellegant,
natty, delectable,
suave, cool, adorable
DAMNED![7]

The Church needs a baptism with the Holy Ghost
and fire, because until then our generation will
throng the gates of hell, because *no man cried for
their souls*.[8]

What an epitaph!

SANCTIFICATION

9/STAYING CLEAN

As ye have therefore received Christ Jesus, so walk ye in him: Rooted and built up in him, and stablished in the faith. . . .

Colossians 2:6–7

Among other things, the Bible is a record of the struggle of twice-born men to live in a world run by the once-born.

A. W. Tozer

Christian perfection is not so severe, tiresome and constraining as we think. It asks us (only) to be God's from the bottom of our hearts.

Francois Fenelon

Many modern Christians have a few vague notions about sanctification which are, at best, haltingly expressed on rare occasions. Sanctification, often viewed as a post salvation doctrine, nearly always fails to carry the theological import of the "basics" such as faith and justification. It has become another one of those "nice, but not necessary" doctrines; a spiritual luxury enjoyed by those dedicated enough to pursue God *after* He has saved them.

Our relationship with Christ entails more than salvation of course, but it also involves more than following Him. It assumes a severance from all other illicit loves. Sanctification, as applied to our love relationship with Jesus (rather than adapted to an impersonal theology), is simply the "how to" of *faithfulness*.

WILL THE STRUGGLE EVER END?

Very few Christians find themselves wrestling with a love for the devil. The likelihood of our being attracted to Satan's person is more remote than Elijah courting Jezebel. He chills us—leaves us cold. This is not only because of his cruel campaign to torment God, but because there is something inherently foul about him.

> Have we not seen this Devil's destructiveness making a bonfire of past, present and future in one mighty conflagration? Smelt him, rancid-sweet? Touched him, slippery-soft? Measured with the eye his fearful shape? Heard his fearful rhetoric? Glimpsed him, sometimes in a mirror, with drooling, greedy mouth, misty ravening eyes and flushed flesh?[1]

We do not love *him*, but he doesn't require our direct worship. He's quite satisfied to remain behind the scenes, bleeding us through his stable of moral harlots. Greed, lust, envy, pride, and a host of others are in his employ. He operates, if you will, as a spiritual pimp. And when one of his "girls" becomes our lover, our attention is focused on the immediate, while his own role is of little concern to us.

The struggle, as we've said before, isn't with the devil. But neither is it with our desire for happiness and pleasure. It's not the "want to" that constitutes sin, but the "choice to." It is the choice to gratify a desire in an illegal manner. It's not the pimp, nor our desire for the girl that dooms us, it's our choice to lie with her. Sin involves turning our loyalties inside out and giving ourselves to harlotry. And as Christians, it involves even more—it is an issue of faithfulness. "As there can be physical adultery, so too there can be unfaithfulness to the divine bridegroom—spiritual adultery."[2] This is where we feel the tension.

Inside we are aware of God's burning love for us. We recognize the great cost in redemption and we have experienced His tender concern in our lives. Yet, as desperately as we want to show our gratitude, as deeply as we want to reciprocate by demonstrating our love for Him, we find, rather embarrassingly, that it is—well, a struggle. We know He is the one for us. No one could possibly love us as He does, and yet, it seems we spend so much time contending with the allurements of other loves. Appearing alternately as passionate desire or the easy way out, temptation entices us to "be filled".

As temptation beckons and seems to say, "You can't resist for long," our response is often deep frustration. "If I really loved Him why am I struggling?" Gordon Olson asks "Is there no let-up from these constant struggles? Is there no point that can be reached in Christian experience when intermittent waverings in our consecration are eliminated, or at least reduced to momentary less passionate departures?"[3] The answer happily is Yes.

CARNAL CHRISTIANITY?

As we further consider the matter of spiritual faithfulness, two very important and interrelated theological theories surface: *Positional Sanctification* and *Carnal Christianity*. Both are widely prescribed today in order to tranquilize spiritual adulterers struggling in the throes of guilt.

Unger's Bible Dictionary gives us an insight into the nature and implications of positional sanctification in its summary statement of the New Testament teaching on the doctrine of sanctification.

> The New Testament presents the doctrine of salvation in three aspects: *positional*, *experiential* and *ultimate*. Positional sanctification is the possession of everyone 'in Christ.' It depends only upon one's union with and position 'in Christ.' First Corinthians presents proof that imperfect believers are nevertheless positionally sanctified and therefore 'saints.' The Corinthian Christians were carnal in life but they are twice said to have been sanctified.[4]

In other words, the Corinthian Christians were *positionally* sanctified without being *experientially* sanctified. Or, according to Scofield's notes, they were *walking* "after the flesh" but were nevertheless "renewed" by the spirit.[5] To help us sort out all of these positions and experiences, consider the passage in question.

> And I, brethren, could not speak unto you as unto spiritual, but as unto carnal, even as unto babes in Christ. I have fed you with milk, and not with meat: for hitherto ye were not able to bear it, neither yet now are ye able. For ye are yet carnal: for whereas there is among you envying, and strife, and divisions, are ye not carnal, and walk as men?
>
> 1 Corinthians 3:1–3

In his book, *What Should We Think of the Carnal Christian?*, Ernest Reisinger relates the following story:

> At a church service that I attended recently, the preacher, a sincere minister, was expounding 1 Corinthians, chapter 3, and he said to a large congregation, 'Now after you become a Christian you have another choice—either to grow in grace, follow the Lord and become a spiritual Christian, or to remain a babe in Christ and live like natural men.' He used 1 Corinthians 3:1–4 to state that there were three categories of men—the *natural* man, the *spiritual* man, and the *carnal* man. He described the carnal man as being like the natural man who was unconverted.[6]

This practice of categorizing men into various spiritual configurations has become extremely popular. Ministers unwilling to offend their congregations, and fearful of being called legalists, have created spiritual pigeonholes to accommodate any and all lifestyles. Reisinger continues,

> One of the most common and popular presentations of this position is available in the form of a small tract which presents the teaching like this:

"After you have invited Christ into your life, it is possible for you to take control of the throne of your life again. The New Testament passage, 1 Corinthians 2:14—3:3, identifies three kinds of people:

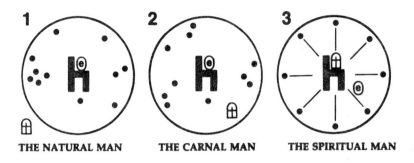

| THE NATURAL MAN | THE CARNAL MAN | THE SPIRITUAL MAN |

h = throne or control center

e = ego or finite self

● = various interests in life

⊞ = Christ, who is either: 1. Outside the life 2. In the life but off the throne

3. In the life and on the throne.

There will be no dispute about the first circle which represents the non-Christian. Note the position of the Ego, indicating that self is on the throne. The natural man is a self-centered man; his interests are controlled by self. Now compare this with the second circle—the only difference is that a cross (representing Christ) appears, although not on the throne. And the same little dots are in circle two as in circle one, indicating that there has been no basic reorganization or change in the nature and character. That is to say, the bent of the life of the 'carnal Christian' is the same as that of the non-Christian. Circle two gives basically the same picture as circle one, the only difference being that the 'carnal Christian' has made a profession of receiving Jesus. But he is 'not trusting God'."[7]

What this teaching essentially propounds is this: If an individual has at some moment in time accepted Christ, he is, from that moment on, positionally sanctified "in Christ." This position he now has in Christ has nothing to do with his day-to-day behavior or experiential sanctification. In other words, it is possible to be positionally sanctified while living carnally. We are not talking here about *doing* carnal things, or having difficulties in a particular area. We are talking about an individual who is *walking* after the flesh, whose ego or self is still on the throne of the heart.

What is the difference between a positionally sanctified, carnal Christian living for himself supremely and an unregenerate, natural man living for himself supremely? Here again we see strong evidence of theology detached from relationship. Unger's Bible Dictionary expounds these confused categories:

> The basis of experiential sanctification, or *actual holiness of life*, is positional sanctification or what one is 'in Christ.' One's position is true *whether or not* he reckons or counts it as true. But it becomes *experientially real* only . . . as one reckons it to be true.[8]

In order to effectively understand any scripture, consideration must be given to the surrounding context in which it lies. When the context of the *carnal Christian* passage is examined, we discover that Paul is dealing with the specific problem of factionalism (unwholesome divisions).

> Paul is not saying that they (the Corinthian believers) were characterized by carnality in every area of their lives. He is not expounding a general doctrine of carnality but reproving a *specific* outcropping of carnality in one certain respect.[9]

If this passage in 1 Corinthians does not establish a special category for loose-living Christians, then where in scripture *do* we find reference to the issue? Where *does* the Bible state that a Christian can live carnally? Where does it say that he can be positionally sanctified without being sanctified experientially? The fact of the matter is that positional sanctification is simply being used as another term for justification, the forgiveness of sins, while experiential sanctification is defined as a nonessential change of heart which takes place in some believers after salvation. This is a serious error.

When the Bible talks about the new covenant (Jeremiah 31:31–34; Ezekiel 36:24–27; Hebrews 10:15–17), it describes

> . . .one covenant with two inseparable parts—the *forgiveness of sins* and *a changed heart*. When a sinner is reconciled to God something happens in the record of heaven, the blood of Christ covers his sins—but at the same time something happens on earth in the heart. The 'carnal Christian' teaching appeals to those who are supposed to be justified, *as though* a new heart and life are optional. Sanctification is spoken of as though it can be subsequent to the forgiveness of sins and so people are led to believe that they are justified even though they are not being sanctified! The truth is that we have no reason to believe that Christ's blood covers our sins in the record of heaven if the Spirit has not changed our hearts on earth. These two great blessings are joined together in the one covenant.[10]

In other words, God can't forgive a man without a transformation.

SPIRITUAL MATURITY— THE "ABIDING" PRINCIPLE

How then are we transformed? How do we stabilize our lives against the turbulence created by appetites and passions accustomed to gratification? Can we in fact reach a place of spiritual maturity? The answers to these questions are worth their weight in gold to Christians in quest of guidelines for victorious Christian living. And happily these answers are available to us.

Spiritual victory is not realized by giving mental assent to an abstract positional theology. Spiritual victory must *involve* us. Yet clearly it

> . . . is not something that we achieve by ourselves in a state of isolation, (nor is it) something that we have as a personal possession. Rather, it is an achieved state of relationship with God.[11]

Or as Charles Finney wrote,

> Our activity, though properly our own, is nevertheless stimulated and directed by His presence and agency within us, so that we can and must say with Paul, 'yet not I, but Christ liveth in me.'[12]

Jesus said:

> He that abideth in me, and I in him, the same bringeth forth much fruit, for without me ye can do nothing.
>
> John 15:5

Not only do these words remind us of what we *cannot do*, they present us with a blueprint for action; they reveal to us what we *can do*. The gospel of John (chapters 15 and 17) supplies us with a definition and instructions for application of the power of God in sanctification.

The word sanctified actually means *set apart*. It is worth noting, however, that the biblical concept of sanctification does not stress being *entirely removed*. It rather conveys the idea of being "different in the midst of" or "in but not of." Jesus prays for His disciples along this very line.

> I do not ask Thee to take them out of the world, but to keep them from the evil one. They are not of the world, even as I am not of the world. Sanctify them in the truth; Thy word is truth. As Thou didst send Me into the world, I also have sent them into the world. And for their sakes I

> sanctify Myself, that they themselves also may be
> sanctified in truth.
>
> John 17:15–19 (NASB)

In an earlier chapter Jesus gives us the practical "how to" of being in the world but not of it. We find the word *abide* appearing ten times in the first ten verses of John chapter 15. Jesus is not offering teaching on salvation here. He is not talking to people who are not sanctified. He is dispensing the secret of *maintaining* our spiritual walk. In John 15:3 Jesus says, "You are already clean because of the word which I have spoken to you." But he immediately then states, "Abide in Me" if you want to produce any spiritual fruit.

> If anyone does not abide in Me, he is thrown away as a branch, and dries up and they gather them, and cast them into the fire, and they are burned.
>
> John 15:6 (NASB)

A branch that is not abiding in the vine is symbolic of a life that is out of relationship with God. And a life out of relationship with God is cut off from the only life source in the universe. This is precisely why this life will dry up.

> The Psalmist could say, 'All my springs are in Thee.' He is the fountain of life. Whatever of life is in us flows directly from Him, as the sap flows from the vine to the branch . . .[13]

> Deliverance from sin as promised in the Gospel is impossible unless we are willing to live a life in communication with God, for it is the Godhead who must deliver us. If we do not want to take the trouble to maintain this happy, submissive life, then we are left to fight our own battles—with gruesome defeat on every hand.[14]

So, in order to remain sanctified or "set apart" from sin and the world, we must abide in Christ. Not in some mystical, abstract manner, but in regular intimate communion with earnest desire.

The experience of abiding in Christ is like being in the eye of a hurricane. As long as our attention is focused on Him, we are kept in perfect peace though the winds of iniquity rage all about us. We are "in but not of." Outside of Christ's embrace, however, we have no more chance of resisting the maelstrom of sin than a leaf in a mid-winter gale. We must be reminded that:

> . . . continual deliverance depends upon our having learned the secret of continual abiding in Christ, and that, therefore, it is not automatic. We must learn not only the 'how' but also the 'when.' Or, to put it more fully, we must not only learn *how* to look to the Lord in faith but must become sharpened in our spiritual perception and sensitivity to the guidance of the Holy Spirit, so that we instantly recognize *when* we need to look to the Lord for deliverance.[15]

> When will the Church understand that Christ is our sanctification; that we have no life, no holiness, no sanctification, except as we abide in Christ . . ."[16]

DEATH IS A DOOR

The question that seems to occur to many at this point concerns the actual initiation and outworking of this "abiding" relationship. Our emotional lives have been cultivated for so long that they have, as Charles Finney stated, become "tremblingly alive" to the things of the world. How is it possible to live in the spiritual realm while our emotional lives are geared to the natural? Jesus gives us the answer.

> Verily, verily, I say unto you, Except a corn of wheat fall into the ground and die, it abideth along: but if it die, it bringeth forth much fruit.
> John 12:24

If it die—it bringeth forth fruit. Jesus, using the analogy of a seed falling to the ground, losing its form and eventually bringing forth fruit, sets forth the spiritual principle of *life from death*. Death, in this case to self, represents a doorway to the spiritual relationship that is referred to as being "in Christ." This relationship is complete when we love Jesus *and* keep His words. Of a man at this stage Jesus states, "My Father will love him, and we will come unto him, and make our abode with him." (John 14:23).

Except it die—it abideth alone. The individual who chooses to hold on and resist the world through *abstinence* rather than *abiding* is fighting a losing battle. We are simply too ill-equipped to conquer sin while abiding alone. Relationship is crucial. As Watchman Nee declares,

> Abstinence is merely worldly. Yet how many earnest Christians are forsaking all sorts of worldly pleasures in the hope thereby of being delivered out of the world! You can build yourself a hermit's hut in some remote spot and think to escape the world by retiring there, but the world will follow you . . . It will dog your footsteps and find you no matter where you hide. Our deliverance from the world begins, not with our giving up this or that but with our seeing, as with God's eyes, that it is a world under sentence of death.[17]

I recall a young man several years ago caught in the grip of an intense inner struggle. Brought up in a Christian home, well versed in doctrine and blessed with a fine intellect, he was nevertheless gripped by spiritual unrest. After spending many days analyzing his situation in hopes of isolating the root of his seeming paralysis, I was on the brink of discouragement when the Lord all at once provided the answer from a most unexpected source. A few days prior, I had been reading a novel about a deadly plague ravaging the Algerian port of Oran. Near the end of the story, the author described the ordeal of one particular man who contacted the plague after working tirelessly as a volunteer in the overloaded hospital. He was striken at a time when it appeared the plague had passed. The account of his struggle to prevent the plague from claiming him as one of its final victims created a poignant drama.

I looked at my friend as the Lord brought the story to my mind and said, "Jerry, you're resisting the Divine Plague! You've been fighting tenaciously to hang on to your life, and God wants you to let it go. He wants you to succumb, Jerry . . . to die!" As long as you fight to retain control of your life, He is unable to possess you and perform all these things you have been asking Him to do in you and through you. I realize it's terrifying to feel the reins of your life slipping from your hands. Death is never easy because it is veiled on the side of the living, and we just don't know what's to become of us.

Until we all are prepared to yield completely, God will faithfully trouble us, as Malcolm Muggeridge suggests in his book *Jesus Rediscovered*.

> God comes padding after me like a Hound of Heaven. His shadow falls over all my little picnics in the sunshine, chilling the air; draining viands of their flavor, talk of its sparkle, desire of its zest . . . one shivers as the divine beast of prey gets ready for the final spring; as the shadow lengthens, reducing to infinite triviality all mortal hopes and desires.[18]

We hang on to our lives tightly because we are afraid of what we will lose should we let them go. This fact is in itself revealing. It shows us what we are really living for. As we waver over the conscious and the tangible, it reveals a short-sighted desire for the immediate. Like the children of Israel seeking a "table in the wilderness," we ask, "Can God provide flesh for His people?"

We find out soon enough that God will give us our own desire. Down it comes, flesh, the tangible something we can sink our teeth into, the immediate. Delighted with our circumstance we "fill" ourselves with that which will never fill us. But in time the euphoria is gone. We discover that the "immediate" looks less real all the time.

We are all, in a sense, like thirsty desert wanderers. It is natural for us to jump at the first "sighting" of desperately needed water. But the wise man will not run after it long. He will not fail to notice that the water which he had spotted and with which he sought to quench his thirst is keeping its fair distance no matter how much ground he covers. Yet today so many are actually increasing the thirst they seek to quench by continually rushing after mirages. Jesus said:

> He that findeth his life shall lose it: and he that loseth his life for my sake shall find it.
>
> Matthew 10:39

God is not attempting to strip away our dreams and ambitions altogether. He is merely trying to encourage us toward that which will really satisfy. He encourages those who "hunger and thirst *after righteousness*" that "they shall be filled." We hear the voice of God across the desert, "Ho, every one that thirsteth, come ye to the waters. . . ." (Isaiah 55:1). The man who "loses" his life doesn't die in the desert chasing mirages, but discovers out of the somewhat frightening, trembling expiration of self, a new, inner oasis.

> But whosoever drinketh of the water that I shall give him shall never thirst; but the water that I shall give him shall be in him a well of water springing up into everlasting life.
>
> John 4:14

Those who will release themselves utterly into the hands of God will discover a sense of abandonment to the things that previously occupied their hearts. It's at once a feeling of near-weightless relief, after the pressure of managing our own affairs is dispensed with, and a sense of being borne up into the heavenlies where life suddenly takes on brand new perspective. We are freed from the burden of governing our own affairs that we might focus our attention on the King's business. Although the process of giving ourselves wholly to God involves giving up our sin as a first step, the matter by no means ends at this point. There is also an emptying involved that drains out all ostensible rights. He will take rightful but loving control over every area of our lives; mere confession of sin is not enough. He does not want us to give up our sins and keep ourselves, He wants us to give up the whole package.

> The Christian way is different: harder and easier. Christ says 'Give Me all. I don't want so much of your time and so much of your money and so much of your work: I want you. I have not come to torment your natural self, but to kill it.[19]

Not yielding up to God what is rightfully His, Fenelon calls "sacrilegious theft." We might even venture to say that holding on to our rights amounts, in effect, to spiritual suicide.

THE ART OF BUILDING YOUR OWN CROSS

The reader might like to get on with dying, but not know how to go about it. It's one thing to have a *willingness* to give up to God what is rightfully His, and quite another to know *how to do it*. I remember receiving a letter not too long ago from a young man begging me to instruct him on how he might die to himself. He was more than willing. He was desirous of the death of his self-interests to bring him into more intimate fellowship with the Lord. He just didn't know how to go about it.

The answer is—*don't do it*. Don't try to set up your own execution. Many Christians interpret Jesus' admonition to "take up the cross" as instructions to begin immediate cross building. This is a mistake. Although Jesus indeed instructs us to take up *our* cross (as opposed to *His* cross— Calvary), He nowhere suggests that we attempt spiritual self-execution. John Wright Follette reminds us,

> The cross is a symbol of suffering. Do you want to live? Then take up your cross. What is your cross? You will have to interpret your own cross, for yours is not like anyone else's. It will be a cross fitting your whole concept and disposition, and more than that, your *will*. Whatever you are *in*

> *your will,* determines your cross. What may be a
> cross to you may seem like a joy-ride to another.
> It is that which will crucify the *I* in you that will
> determine your cross . . ."[20]

Why can't we build our own crosses? Simply because the ones we build do not get the job done. No one is proficient at self-execution. For this reason, when an individual attempts to "crucify" himself, more often than not, he remains very much alive. A cross manufactured by a twentieth-century Christian is generally quite plush. Padded and cushioned, the believer reposes on the cross in style. To help ease the pain, sympathetic friends mount a special remote control television set and pass up a sponge filled with Coca-Cola. Within a few days the "disciple" dismounts his cross and begins to share on the resurrection life, of which he knows nothing—due, of course, to the fact he never died!

If we will wait on the Lord, He will, master craftsman that He is, fashion a cross for us that will accomplish its purpose. It will slay us. He knows what it will take to bring us to the end:

> He disillusions us with ourselves by the experi-
> ence of our weakness and our corruption, in an
> infinite number of failures, and yet, even then
> when He seems to overwhelm us, it is for our
> good, it is to spare us from the harm which we
> would do to ourselves. What we weep for would
> have made us weep eternally. What we believe to
> have lost was lost when we thought we had it.[21]

It was only a desert mirage.

SEEING EYES

Spiritual victory is realized only when we see the path of life from a higher position. An earthly view alone is too localized and deceptive. Although the immediate view may be *accurate*, it is nevertheless *limited*. We can only garner the strength to refuse the compromises of immediate pleasures by acquiring a full *and* accurate view of life, the sort of "extended vision" which gave Moses the strength to forsake the temporal pleasures of Pharaoh's palace. ". . . He endured, as seeing Him who is invisible" (Heb. 11:27). When Elisha and his young servant were surrounded by hostile forces, the prophet said,

> Lord, I pray thee, open his eyes that he may see. And the Lord opened the eyes of that young man; and he saw: and behold, the mountain was full of horses and chariots of fire round about Elisha.
>
> 2 Kings 6:17

Our tendency to think pessimistically seems to affect our outlook on just about everything. Religious themes are not only *not exempted* from this pessimism, they are prime targets. This matter of dying to self is a good example of what I mean. It seems the only thing many people can think of when this subject is broached is what they will have to give up, what they are going to lose. Yet God promises that 'He that loses his life for my sake will find it." He will find his life! What encouraging tidings! These are not negative words of loss, but positive words. Jesus offers no *equation* here. Rather, He offers us life for mere existence, and extended vision for spiritual blindness. It is an offer made by One who knows what living really is, to those who do not. The Master's words contain no paradox except to those limited by a "flesh and blood" worldview.

In other words, this "extended vision" is a direct reward of this process of spiritual death. Job evidently acquired "seeing eyes" after his cross had done its work, for he declared, "I have heard of thee by the hearing of the ear but now mind eye seeth thee" (Job 42:5).

"Blessed are the pure in heart: for they shall see God" (Matthew 5:8). Those diligent enough to see God will see, as well, the overall structure of life. It's not that this structure is invisible that so many fail to see it, but that spiritual blindness is so widespread. Life cannot be accurately interpreted by anyone other than a true Christian. This is true not because Christians have necessarily earned positions of counsel, but because they "see." God has designed that spiritual sight be a possession of the humble. Thus it is that those unwilling to "lose their lives" for His sake are destined to remain blind.

So often those involved in various spiritual projects are totally oblivious to the place and purpose of their particular vision in God's overall scheme. They work at it day after day with no real understanding of what they are doing. The man of God, however, who has lost his life for Christ's sake, who has fallen into the ground and died, receives his commission from the Lord along with its context. He arises from his "death" to view the world through eyes that see color and detail which the church's leisure class fails to notice. To this man life vibrates with meaning and anticipation.

> I am a flame born of celestial fire
> I bear a name, Insatiable Desire.
> I wear in heart an image all divine,
> Past human art, not traced by mortal line.
> I hear God call to taste His heavenly power,
> I give my all to burn life's single hour.
> So let me burn through fetters that would bind;
> Thus will I learn and freedom will I find.
> I shall return to Love's eternal fire.
> There shall I burn—a satisfied desire.[22]

May we pursue a clean heart and righteous hands within the diligence of a David. May we return to Love's eternal fire and hear him say, "Blessed are your eyes, for they see. . . . " (Matt. 13:16).

EVANGELISM

10/SPREAD THE GOOD WORD

Declare His glory among the heathen, his wonders among all people.

Psalm 96:3

The Church was not designed to be a reservoir, ever-receiving and retaining for itself God's spiritual blessings, but rather a conduit conveying them on and out to others everywhere.

Robert Hall Glover

That which is considered lowly, small and worthless, madness to the world . . . these God chose; in them is the richness of life. Giver of miracles, Sustainer of life: the fish, the birds, the trees, I want to praise You. Remain as my strength so I will be able to tell others.

Finnish School Song

In 1973 I was arrested along with several friends in downtown Moscow by the Soviet KGB. The situation developed following an impromptu worship gathering. During the course of my subsequent interrogation, I was emphatically informed there were churches available for the purpose of discussing matters of a religious nature. Following this highly debatable assertion, my interrogators wished to. know why I felt it necessary to share my message on the crowded Red Square. I felt their real question had gone unasked: Why must you share at all? Why have you come to our country to share your own subjective religious experience?

Why had I indeed? What is the rationale behind a decision to travel thousands of miles to share a personal, subjective experience? This is truly something we need to settle in our own hearts before we can approach evangelism with any appreciable zeal. Every year countless hours and enormous sums of money are expended in evangelistic endeavors by Christians who have never asked themselves this essential question, let alone answered it.

THE PHILOSOPHY OF EVANGELISM

Not a day passes but that the world is discovering the frustration that results in attempting to understand Christian activity apart from Christian teaching. To my Soviet interrogators, my faith was an incorporeal experience and nothing more. It wasn't difficult for me, knowing their definition, to understand their amazement over my actions.

The point is that Christianity is *more* than an experience. Many Christian people in their haste to spread their joy, relate a subjective experience rather than objective truths. While this is a great deal safer (in that people do not seem nearly as threatened by personal experience), it is also infinitely less productive than the presentation of objective, invasive truths.

The essence of Christ's great commission rests in what He has *taught* us, not what He has *done* for us (important and precious as this is). Only Christ's teaching can work a similar inner miracle in another's life. If what we share with the world is solely a subjective experience, we run the risk of seeing it routinely tossed into the world's ever-growing bag of experiences. The only factor that sets the Christian experience apart from Krishna-consciousness, spiritism, existentialism or what-have-you, is the intrinsic truth of Christianity.

However, a philosophy of evangelism must encompass more than *what* we share; it must include the *why*. Why do we share? There appear to be two reasons why every Christian needs to share the Gospel message with others: *obedience* and *life purpose*. Although the two are linked together in the sense that obedience is the life purpose of every Christian, our immediate design is to examine the philosophy of evangelism from both an objective and a subjective standpoint.

Sharing Christ's Word in Obedience

Samuel Zwemer once remarked, "If evangelical Christianity is reducible to a successful communication of a valuable experience, we need no theology of missions. But the New Testament makes perfectly clear that the aim of Christian missions is the fulfillment of a Divine Command. . ."[1] This Divine Command, known as "The Great Commission," is found in each of the first five books of the New Testament.

Matthew
And Jesus came up and spoke to them, saying, 'All authority has been given to Me in heaven and on earth. *Go therefore and make disciples of all the nations,* baptizing them in the name of the Father and the Son and the Holy Spirit, teaching them to observe all that I commanded you; and lo, I am with you always, even to the end of the age.'
Matthew 28:18–20 (NASB)

Mark
And He said to them, *'Go into all the world and preach the gospel to all creation.'*
Mark 16:15 (NASB)

Luke
And He said to them, 'thus it is written . . . that repentance for forgiveness of sins should be *proclaimed in His name to all the nations. . . .*"
Luke 24:46–47 (NASB)

John
Jesus therefore said to them again, 'Peace be with you; *as the Father has sent Me, I also send you.'*
John 20:21 (NASB)

Acts
But you shall receive power when the Holy Spirit has come upon you; and *you shall be My witnesses both in Jerusalem, and in all Judea and Samaria, and even to the remotest part of the earth.*
Acts 1:8 (NASB)

The words of our Lord in Acts take on even greater impact when we realize they were His very last words on earth. While this may seem incidental to some, the subject was evidently important enough to Jesus to occupy His final thoughts.

There is in these great commission scriptures an unmistakable command—*Go*. As Loren Cunningham reminds us, "Go means a change of location." Jesus' promise that He would be with us to the end of the world is linked to His command to "Go." The extent of Christ's "Go" in our lives depends solely on His purposes at any given time. Every true Christian understands "he is not his own" and that therefore personal plans are not to detain us against Christ's call. Many times when we say we don't *feel a leading*, we are really saying we don't have a *feeling*.

Our absolute obedience to Christ is a manifestation of our absolute love for Him. We don't go into the world proclaiming the gospel in order to impress each other with our dedication. We do not go out of a sense of sterile obligation. But neither do we go primarily because we feel such compassion for the lost. No, we do not go for *their* sakes—we go for *His* sake, because Jesus Christ deserves to have what He died for. As His servants, we obey His commission of love to go to the ends of the earth in search of a bride. No nation or city, village or island must be forgotten, no street or field overlooked. She is everywhere, and He wants her. We must fetch her.

Sharing Christ's Love As Our Purpose for Living

Proverbs tells us, "Where there is no vision, the people perish. . . ." (Proverbs 29:18). The Hebrew word for perish in this scripture is *para*, which literally means "to cast off restraint." The picture this suggests is marvelous. Our vision consists of the revealed plan of God for our lives during any given period. God's plans are not, as some appear to think, coloring books in which He supplies a general outline and we fill in the detail according to our discretion. A God-given vision is pregnant with detail. The general outline is there, but He also supplies us with detailed instructions regarding the colors He wants.

I am frequently approached by confused believers beset with discouragement and frustration. I generally get around to asking, "Well, what is your vision?" More often than not there is no answer—and that *is* the answer—for where there is no vision the people perish (cast off restraint). Let me illustrate it this way: The will of God for our lives, the specific, tailored purpose for our lives, our vision, becomes as it were the walls of a conduit or pipe. As such, it performs a constraining and a restraining function. Characteristically it channels our life's energy and flow to a prescribed end, while at the same time prevents our thoughts and energies from dissipating arbitrarily and prematurely into useless stagnant puddles.

The frustrated Christians had become stagnant puddles. They weren't going anywhere. Because they had no vision they had cast off the restraining qualities of the will of God. Their life's energies were spewing out of gaping holes in the pipe. When God desires to accomplish some task through them and turns on the faucet, nothing happens— there is no longer any water pressure. Instead of allowing the will of God to channel their lives in an energetic, purposeful fashion, they have become shallow, stagnant pools of aimless inactivity.

I'LL KEEP GOD TO MYSELF

It is impossible for men to 'settle' in the world completely without God. Although proud of its successes and attainments, the world sees, every day, more clearly the provisional and insufficient nature of its civilization. On the verge of having its foundations shaken to the core, it thirsts as never before for the true Light.

But the most surprising fact in modern spiritual life must be considered our indifference toward this thirst, our own too-easy consent to the division existing between the Church and the world. We refuse to recognize that this external division is supported not only by the 'willfulness of the world,' but also by our own stagnant Christianity . . . is it not we ourselves who have helped to reduce the meaning of the life of the Church to an 'intimate little corner' of piety locked away with seven locks from the life of the world?[2]

This is a picture of the ultra-sophisticated, twentieth-century shrine. It is Sunday—the feast day of the fellowship. All across the land we gather to spend our time and count our blessings. Huddled together in our insulated environments we take great care to avoid letting the heat out, or the cold in. We only want warm bodies, it's much too difficult to warm a cold one.

How vividly I recall an incident shared by Floyd McClung, so indicative of our demise. A pastor delivered the following account:

> A couple days ago on my way to the Church I noticed a pathetic-looking young girl. She was standing forlornly in front of a halfway house which had evidently been closed. It was a bitterly cold day and she was shivering in her scanty clothes. Probably she wasn't much over 16 years old and yet, there she was cradling a dirty, little baby in her arms—obviously looking for help. My heart was touched as I drove by.

We simply don't want to bring a draft into our warm fellowships . . . but our hearts are touched.

> We have gotten used to 'owning' our Christianity and keeping it to ourselves, to not sharing it, as if it were an accidental inheritance.[3]

Thus we have the Fraternal Christian Club, a place to be among one's own. Fellowship becomes the excuse we use to keep God to ourselves. The Bible tells us, "If anyone does not have the Spirit of Christ, he does not belong to Him" (Romans 8:9). That spirit was 'to seek and to save that which was lost'. Where do we get the idea that we can close the sheepfold to all but the warm, attractive sheep? What was Jesus really saying to Peter (and to us) when He closed the book of John with the words "Feed my sheep"? (John 21:15–17). The popular interpretation is that Jesus' sheep represent only Christians. Perhaps we ought to look again.

> But when he saw *the multitudes,* he was moved
> with compassion on them, because they fainted,
> and were scattered abroad, as *sheep* having no
> shepherd."
>
> Matthew 9:36

"The world might rather take offense at the Church for keeping the secret of salvation to itself and being unable or unwilling to speak about it in accessible language."[4] This possessive, self-indulgent mentality that so subtly, yet so powerfully grips the Church today, will one day be judged.

A BRIDE'S DISCRETION

Overfed
and underbred
the Church has gone astray
a harlot's bed
the prophets said
would hasten her decay
what does she care
about an empty chair
at a wedding feast he's planned
values rotted
garments spotted
the bride has spoiled his day

She revels in her merrymaking
doesn't care his heart is breaking
won't someone speak to her?

She fraternized
rationalized
her children do the same
clutching lies
they roll their eyes
disdaining thought of blame
they spend their worth
in pursuit of mirth
mortgaging empty souls
all that's left
from Satan's theft
are orphans with their shame

Who would've dreamed she'd give him up
to taste the wine from Satan's cup
is there nothing we can do?

Destitute
the prostitute
has left her brood alone
her body's fruit
will follow suit
in bolting heaven's home
but she cannot conceal
what time will reveal
they're illegitimate posterity
in willing him part
they sealed their hearts
forgetting his home is a throne

Abdication
through resignation
morality has no creed
the congregation
of the nation
relinquishes her lead
a careless choice
to lose one's voice
while hell is growing bold
but all that mattered
drowned in chatter
as ecumenicals agreed

She revels in her merrymaking
doesn't care his heart is breaking
won't someone speak to her?

Can a maid forget her ornaments, or a bride her
attire? yet my people have forgotten me days
without number. Why trimmest thou thy way to
seek love? therefore hast thou also taught the
wicked ones thy ways.

Jeremiah 2:32–33

> The Church is in her Babylonian captivity, and as
> Israel could not sing the songs of Zion in a
> strange land, so Christians in bondage have no
> authoritative message to declare.
>
> A.W. Tozer

A KINGDOM NOT OF THIS WORLD

In Evgeny Barabanov's brilliant essay, "The Schism Between the Church and the World," he establishes a fundamental flaw in the thinking of the Russian Church (and to my mind, in the Western Church as well) which left the door ajar to humanistic activists:

> Heavenward aspirations often went hand in hand
> with execration of the earth. Too often the ideal of
> salvation was built on a foundation of inflexible
> renunciation of this world. Thus salvation itself
> was understood as an escape from the material
> world into a world of pure spirituality.[5]

The Soviet State had a message for the Church, and it came in the form of a cynical resolution by the Soviet Central Committee:

> You say you are not of this world, well then,
> there is nothing for you to do in this world.[6]

Perhaps this is a message the Church wants to hear. It would certainly appear that way when one observes her extreme reticence to handle any of the burning issues of our day. The primary line of reasoning is that admitting political and social issues into the Church tends to encourage factionalism, which in turn erodes unity. I quite agree when no clear biblical guideline is evident, but there are plenty of clear-cut issues on which the Church must take a stand.

Be that as it may, there is one thing of which we may be certain: If we do not want to be involved in this world, there are scores of godless people who will gladly take our political and social "burdens" from us. With responsibility goes authority; by abdicating our responsibilities, we in turn lose our voice and authority in the world. The Church's message to the humanistic princes of this world has been clear—"You go ahead and run things. Just let us go on with our fellowship." This "drop out" mentality was noted by Bob Dylan in his hit song "Desolation Row":

> Ophelia she's 'neath the window
> for her I feel so afraid
> on her twenty-second birthday
> she already is an old maid
> to her death is quite romantic
> she wears an iron vest
> her profession's her religion
> her sin is her lifelessness.[7]

What a travesty that the Church of Jesus Christ should be indicted for lifelessness! Our detachment from this world has made a mockery of our message. Perhaps our callousness stems from our obliviousness, but perhaps not. The fact remains, according to the words of Christ, that a Christian is one not only called *out* of the world but sent back *into* the world as well. Certainly the good news of Christianity is not limited to the world beyond the grave.

Recently I observed two women engaged in a strange, new Christian ritual. They'd spent quite some time discussing the miserable state of the world, fuming over this and fretting about that—all the while gesticulating their distress in a most remarkable manner. Eventually, just prior to wrapping up the solemn conversation, they slapped each other on the back and asked with enormous smiles, "Aren't you glad Jesus is coming to take us out of this mess?"

This longing for "home" affects us all at times, and there is assuredly nothing wrong with this. That is, until we become so intoxicated by other-worldly thinking that we neglect to maintain the present. Malcolm Muggeridge put it this way: "I often pined for total detachment from a society whose standards I despise and whose future prospects I regard as catastrophic, but in which I, nonetheless, have an inescapable stake."[8]

How many times has it happened that an athletic team has found a weak opponent scheduled prior to some important contest, and wound up getting beaten? They had their minds on future matters while their bodies were trying to conduct present business.

Jesus said we were to be *in the world* but not *of* it. He said we were to *be the salt* of the earth. He said we were *to occupy* until He returned—so let's get on with it! Let's occupy territory for the kingdom of God. Let's work on preserving our society from wanton destruction by actively pursuing and demonstrating righteousness. We are behind in a game we ought to be winning!

MANNEQUINS, POPCORN AND CHEER

Those of you who are scratching your heads, asking what in the world this heading means, need some explanation.

If we are going to conquer this world for Christ, there are three points to remember: we must allow Him to speak for Himself; we must let Him do what He wants; and we must do what He says. If the following illustration will help you to remember these three ingredients, it will have served its purpose.

Definition: Mannequin—

> Something which allows you to create appearance
> and display your own tastes.

One would almost think from the looks of things these days that Jesus Christ owns the biggest wardrobe in town. Everyone from the liberal theologian trying to legitimize homosexuality, to the local youth pastor trying to prove the great commission means halloween parties, have an outfit in which they feel Jesus looks especially nice. Church board meetings, Jesus rock concerts, revival meetings, encounter groups—you name it—after the program kickoff, Jesus will inevitably appear to rubber-stamp His support of any and all activities. So today, as if Jesus could no longer speak for Himself, He is wheeled onto platforms, into meetings, used anywhere His name might be helpful in legitimizing men's deeds. Everybody's "dressin' up" Jesus.

How ludicrous it is to think we can force Jesus into our garments. Jesus Christ can never be a mannequin, for a mannequin is at the mercy of the clothing designer and Jesus chooses His own clothes. In addition (for the benefit of those who didn't know), Jesus only owns one suit. . .

> And He is clothed with a robe dipped in blood; and His name is called the Word of God. . . .
>
> And on His robe and on His thigh He has a name written, *"KING OF KINGS, AND LORD OF LORDS.*
>
> Revelation 19:13,16 (NASB)

To present Jesus Christ dressed any other way is to present a false Christ. He will only be who he is, He will only speak for Himself. Let us, each one, temper our words accordingly.

Definition: Popcorn—

> Something which makes the main attraction that much more enjoyable.

We in the West are living in a system designed to provide material satisfaction. This system, as Alvin Toffler points out, is generating "experience makers" and "creating an economy geared to the provision of psychic gratification."[9] The more "in-depth" the experience, the better. In other words, an experience involving three senses is preferable to that which stimulates only two. The search is on for the total, sensual-immersion experience.

One of the leading experience manufacturers today is the movie industry. Hollywood launches lavish productions, costing millions of dollars, on a regular basis. The only drawback seems to be that although they're veritable feasts for the eyes and ears (and thanks to Sensurround, the touch), the olfactory nerves and taste buds are unimpressed.

Ah, but not for long! Accommodating as they are, proprietors of movie theaters across the land have solved the problem. The first thing that meets the eye in almost every theater one enters any more is a glass or plastic cubicle sitting atop a concessions counter with the words, *"hot, salty, buttered popcorn"* emblazened across the front. At an additional cost (usually about double the price of your ticket), you can experience the thrill of titillating all your senses simultaneously. Bear in mind, however, that despite the cost, the popcorn itself is not the main attraction. It rather serves to make the main attraction just a little bit more enjoyable.

What folly to think that the King of the universe would consent to cater to our selfishness, that he would provide religious seasoning in order to make our cuisine of self-indulgence palatable.

Jesus Christ is not the *main* attraction in our lives. He is the *only* attraction. He lives in us, He is all of us—everything we do, everything we say, everything we are. He does what He wants to with our lives. This is why He will reject every effort we make to incorporate Him as an appendage to our lifestyles; even if that appendage is disguised as the major thrust of our lives!

Definition: Cheer—

> Something an observer does to feel like a participant.

During my high school years, I indulged in the American craze known as football. In the Los Angeles City School System where I played (and studied a little), the fellows became varsity or B-level players depending on their "exponents" (a combination of age, height and weight). Due to my not-so-massive frame, I played on the "B" team. Since our game was played prior to the varsity contest, this afforded us the opportunity to both play and watch football every Friday night.

As a general rule the fellows on the "B" team would sit together in the bleachers and root for the varsity. I must admit that in spite of our volume and enthusiasm, we never influenced the outcome of the game. It seems strange that one could feel so much like a participant and yet in actuality be so impotent to effect any results. But just being in the proximity and atmosphere of the action wasn't enough. The only fellows truly influencing the outcome of the game were the dirty, weary players down on the field.

An analogous situation exists in Christendom today. This contest is between the forces of heaven and the powers of darkness. The stakes are far higher, however, when you consider the value of a human soul.

Every Sunday the evangelical bleachers fill with eager believers. The cheering section is even replete with cheerleaders in the form of choir directors, associate pastors and song leaders. When the music begins, we sing "I Surrender All," when in actuality we offer very little, or "He Is Lord" when He is not. Somehow we can feel the tide of the battle turning when we sing "Onward, Christian Soldiers" in spite of the fact "Protestant churches have long ago become like N.A.T.O., a headquarters without an army."[10]

WHY SIT WE HERE UNTIL WE DIE?

There is an interesting story in the book of 2 Kings that speaks in the simplest of terms to the deteriorating situation of an ailing Church. Ben-Hadad, the king of Syria, had decided to besiege Samaria. If one possesses sufficient patience, laying siege can be a very effective military tactic. Often it involves nothing more than encircling a fortified position and waiting. In time, supply routes are cut, and the enemy will either starve or surrender.

The whole operation actually went quite well for Ben-Hadad. This becomes evident when you scan the menu inside the city:

Donkey's Head . . . . 80 shekels (silver)
One Pint of Dove's Dung . . . . 5 shekels (silver)
Boiled Sons . . . . no price mentioned

The situation was bleak for the inhabitants of Samaria.

Numbered among the residents of the city were four leprous men who sat at the entrance of the gate. Given their perspective at the time, life's silver lining was pretty tattered. As they looked outside the city, they saw the Syrian army perched like vultures awaiting their prey. Inside the city, starvation had taken its toll and panic was beginning to set in. Then, as they tried to cover their eyes from the sight, they were reminded of their own leprous, decaying flesh. Finally, motivated by desperation, they came to that pivot point where one realizes things are not going to improve and, for better or for worse, decided to "do something". They asked themselves, "Why sit we here until we die?"

Perhaps for the Church of Jesus Christ, standing in the twilight of a spent civilization, it is high time we ask ourselves the same question. A fatalistic, apocalyptic policy of *laissez-faire* doesn't seem quite in order while society is decaying and collapsing around us. Do we doubt that society is collapsing? In light of the ample visual and statistical evidence available today, it is doubtful that anyone other than a naive idealist or fanatic optimist could believe it is not. Nevertheless, the question remains: Just how bad do things have to get before we take action? Are we waiting until our nation is completely trampled into dust—until we are ultimately and utterly consumed? Why sit *We* here until we die?

When you read further in this biblical account, it's interesting to note that four desperate lepers discovered that God had driven the Syrians out of their camp. God had spoken earlier through Elisha concerning the release that was to come, but the officialdom would have none of it.

> Then Elisha said, 'Listen to the word of the LORD; thus says the LORD, "Tomorrow about

> this time a measure of fine flour shall be sold for a
> shekel, and two measures of barley for a shekel,
> in the gate of Samaria." And the royal officer on
> whose hand the king was leaning answered the
> man of God and said, 'Behold, if the Lord should
> make windows in heaven, could this thing be?'
> Then he said, 'Behold you shall see it with your
> own eyes, but you shall not eat of it.'
>
> 2 Kings 7:1–2 (NASB)

The cynical unbelief of the royal officer became his death sentence. Unlike the four lepers who had also concluded the situation was nearly terminal, he neglected to add two vitally important ingredients to the situation—*hope* and *action*. Did not the word of the Lord through the prophet Elisha provide sufficient grounds for the exercise of faith and the manifestation of hope?

When we respond to the Word of the Lord with hope and action, we will surely live to see His deliverance. If, on the other hand, we allow circumstances to foster *unbelief,* then we shall perish.

> So the people went out and plundered the camp
> of the Syrians. Then a measure of fine flour was
> sold for a shekel and two measures of barley for a
> shekel, according to the word of the Lord. Now
> the king appointed the royal officer on whose
> hand he leaned to have charge of the gate; but the
> people trampled on him at the gate, and he died
> just as the man of God had said. . . .
>
> 2 Kings 7:16–17 (NASB)

In the New Testament this same issue is addressed in Jesus' parable of the pounds (Matthew 25:14). Jesus, speaking of Himself, describes a certain nobleman who prepares to leave on a long journey. He gathers his servants together in order to deliver parting instructions. As they stand before him he gives pounds (or talents) to each one with the command, *"Occupy till I come."*

Eventually the nobleman returns to reckon with his servants. One has gained ten pounds, another five. Yet another comes with the word that his pound is wrapped up in a napkin and safely hidden. The master is delighted with the productivity of the first servants. The last servant, however, is a different matter. His report ignites the nobleman's fury.

Why was the master angry? What was the basic difference between the first servants and the last? I think it can be summed up in a word—*inactivity*. He simply didn't do anything with his pound. He had somehow failed to understand, or more likely failed to act upon, his master's instructions to "Occupy till I come." The consequences were severe.

> And cast ye the unprofitable servant into outer darkness: There shall be weeping and gnashing of teeth.
>
> Matthew 25:30

The Master's servants still have difficulty interpreting His instruction today. Many seem to be convinced that it means, "Occupy this church pew until the Lord returns." It has become simply a matter of obtaining our salvation, wrapping it up nicely in religious trappings and waiting. "Suffocating indifference" is the way Leonard Ravenhill put it:

> We Christians are so willfully smug to the lostness of men! We are chronically lazy and so callously indifferent! As lax, loose, lustful and lazy Laodiceans, we are challenging God to spew us out of His mouth.[11]

Who will release the prisoners of the earth? Alexander Solzhenitsyn in a recent, smoldering editorial asked this poignant question: "Do we have the freedom of indifference to a distant alien's trampled freedom?"[12] Consider the following scripture before you answer.

> Deliver those who are being taken away to death, and those who are staggering to slaughter, O hold them back. If you say, 'See, we did not know

> this,' does He not consider it who weighs the hearts? And does He not know it who keeps your soul? And will He not render to man according to his work?
>
> Proverbs 24:11 (NASB)

Solzhenitsyn continues:

> In keeping silent about evil, in burying it so deep within us that no sign of it appears on the surface, we are *implanting* it, and it will rise up a thousand-fold in the future.[13]

> If we wait for history to present us with freedom and other precious gifts, we risk waiting in vain. History is us—and there is no alternative but to shoulder the burden of what we so passionately desire and bear it out of the depths.[14]

A MYSTERIOUS ARMY

Our generation has probably had more than its share of revolution. It doesn't really matter whether you study the "professionals," a la Lenin, Mao and Castro, or the special interest terrorist groups, be they German, Japanese, Italian or Palestinian—the results are identical. Revolution begins with a barrage of inflamed rhetoric and ends with bloodshed and tyranny. When the dust has finally settled, one tyranny has replaced another in the name of progress.

Karl Marx said that "Philosophers have only interpreted the world differently; the point is, however, to change it." The fact remains that neither Marx nor his successors approached the problem of changing the world with enough force. Their weapons of destruction, both ideological and military, were (and still are) far too feeble. All the apparatuses of war in any nation's arsenal are just as capable of being destroyed as they are of destroying. Furthermore, as history has proven, one ruler's ideology is vulnerable to being replaced by the next. In order to change this world, it's going to take a force that is not of this world.

Such a force exists. God is raising up a mysterious army unlike any of which the Pentagon or the Kremlin have ever dreamed. It is unique, powerful, growing, but it is not new. It cannot be stopped by any weapon or barrier known to man. It is relentless and determined. There are no conscripts in this army, it is entirely volunteer. It is an army made up of the dead . . . who are all very much alive.

I shall not give the impression that the princes of this world are afraid or unable to make war against this army, but it can't be destroyed. Trifling with this heavenly army becomes a study in frustration. The enemy dispatches one soldier and ten more spring up in his place. As I mentioned to a Soviet lieutenant in 1973, the repressive regimes of the world would be wise to take notes from history, for whenever the Church has been persecuted, that is precisely when it has flourished. The blood of martyrs has always been the seed of the Church. It has been estimated that for every Christian that perished in the Roman coliseum there were twelve to sixteen new converts in the stands. It's like trying to put out a fire by dousing it with gasoline. The most effective action against this army is *no* action.

> I am crucified with Christ: nevertheless I live; yet
> not I, but Christ liveth in me. . . .
>
> Galatians 2:20

As one surveys the life of our Lord Jesus, the magnitude of His accomplishments cannot help but diminish all tendency toward self-congratulatory conversation. Jesus accomplished infinitely more in just thirty-three years than most of us could hope to conclude in a full lifetime. As J. Oswald Sanders observed, "He spent His time doing things that mattered."[15]

In Jesus' High Priestly Prayer, there are recorded for us some of the most thrilling words in the entire Bible.

> I have glorified thee on the earth: I have finished
> the work which thou gavest me to do.
>
> John 17:4

These words are an example to us. I wonder how many of us, were we to be ushered before the throne of God today, could make such a statement? Let us order our lives in such a way that we might one day experience the deep, eternal satisfaction of repeating these words of Jesus before our Father.

We end by posing C. S. Lewis' question, from his book *Mere Christianity:* "One soul in the whole creation you do know: and it is the only one whose fate is placed in your hands. If there is a God, you are, in a sense, alone with Him. You cannot put Him off with speculations about your next-door neighbors, or memories of what you have read in books. What will all that chatter and hearsay count (will you even be able to remember it?) when the anaesthetic fog which we call 'nature' or 'the real world' fades away, and the Presence in which you have always stood becomes palpable, immediate, and unavoidable?"

STUDY QUESTIONS

Chapter One

1. What is *the* primary necessity if we are to experience an intimate, personal relationship?
2. Give several reasons why an individual may not want to pursue godly understanding.
3. What conclusion can we draw about God if it is true that knowledge decreases faith?
4. What are the two ingredients of true unity? What is the basic cause of disunity?
5. What does it mean to "neglect" so great a salvation?
6. Why did God create man?
7. Give several evidences that would prove God has not endeavored to remain mysterious and aloof.
8. Explain the statement "no man is deceived unless he wants to be deceived" in relation to truth and salvation. Include statements about the two universal sources of moral enlightenment.
9. What is the basic difference between the deceived, the deceivers and the reconciled?
10. In Jesus' parable of the sower, what is the sole difference between the man who is lost and the individual whose life bears fruit?
11. Using the surrounding context, explain what God is saying in Isaiah 55:8-9 regarding His thoughts and ways.
12. What is wrong with defining God's expressed feelings in the Bible as anthropopathisms?

13. What is deficient about a desire to merely "experience" God?
14. Describe the differences between God's being and His character.
15. Which is more important to understand prior to relational committal: physical prowess or character traits?

Chapter Two

1. What is God's expressed standard for His children?
2. Name the two options open to those individuals whose lives do not correspond to the biblical standard.
3. Give a brief definition of holiness.
4. Why is God holy?
5. On what basis does God require us to choose Him supremely?
6. Define the relationship between our supreme, subordinate and simple choices. Which level does God evaluate to determine what is virtuous and what is sinful?
7. What is the difference between Christ's righteousness imputed as a *technicality* versus as a *reality*?
8. Explain the relationship between motive and conduct. What is the meaning of James 4:17?
9. Is it possible to live supremely for God and yourself simultaneously? Give scriptural evidence for your answer.
10. What is moral character?

Chapter Three

1. What is the inherent danger in referring to sin as a sickness?
2. Is sin itself a physical or a moral phenomena?
3. If it is true that men can't obey God, then why should they be disturbed that they aren't?
4. What are some of the weaknesses of the federal head-

ship theory? What is the overriding message of Ezekiel 18?

5. What exactly did Jesus come to earth to save us from?

6. What is wrong with the idea that the only difference between the Christian and non-Christian lifestyle is *forgiveness?*

7. Why can there be no ignorance involved in sin? Give scriptural references.

8. Why does the Bible state that prior to salvation *all* our deeds, "good" and bad, are as filthy rags? Explain Matthew 7:17–18.

9. What is the origin of the sinful nature spoken of in passages such as Ephesians 2:3? How do our thoughts and choices ultimately become our destiny?

10. What is wrong with allowing our minds to become harnessed to our emotions?

Chapter Four

1. Briefly summarize man's situation apart from God.

2. What were the four major difficulties God needed to overcome through the atonement?

3. Was it possible for God to accomplish many ends with just one action?

4. Explain God's governmental problems in reconciliation. How did His problem correspond to Darius'?

5. What does law without sanctions amount to?

6. What thoughts entered Adam's mind about God subsequent to his initial sin? How has this erroneous concept been carried on down through human history?

7. How is this wrong concept transferred to various interpretations of Christ's work in the atonement?

8. Why did God's love not need to be restored by any propitiation? Was the cross of Christ a stimulus to bring mercy about, or an expression of God's predisposition to mercy?

9. What is wrong with the statement, "God is a God of love but He is also a God of justice?"

10. Define the two types of justice. Which type allowed for forgiveness?

11. Define "forgiveness." Why is it impossible to both receive payment on a claim and to forgive it?

12. If the atonement satisfied retributive justice to the tiniest iota, what prospect are we faced with in relation to the Trinity? Where in the universe, if this theory be true, can we find an example of true agape love?

13. Can God relate to man in intimate fellowship when that man thinks he's something he's not? Why is it important for man to see himself as he truly is in the matter of reconciliation?

14. Explain God's motivational problem in reconciliation. What was the key to *maintaining* the relationship against the magnetism of former, inflamed appetites and habit patterns?

15. Do we possess any alluring qualities at all which would attract God to us prior to salvation?

Chapter Five

1. Give several reasons why the atonement could *not* have consisted in Christ's obedience to the moral law on behalf of sinners.

2. What is the difference between an allegory and a metaphor? What is important for us to remember about biblical analogies using transactionary terminology?

3. Could redemption have involved Christ offering his blood as a legal "ransom" to God in order to get Him to release us? Explain.

4. Explain the sense in which our salvation *did* cost something.

5. If it is true that Jesus *literally paid* for our sins with His blood (a paid debt no longer being a debt), and He died for the sins of the whole world, what conclusions must we come to? What is the theological word for it?

6. What is a "limited" atonement? Is it taught in the Bible?

7. Why is it not possible that our salvation was secured through Christ suffering *punishment?* Explain the

potential difference between suffering and punishment.
8. What was the function of the Old Testament sacrificial system? What did the sacrifices *not* represent?
9. Why was it important that the sacrificial animal be without spot or blemish?
10. What does "blood" symbolize in the Bible? What is its importance relative to the atonement?
11. What is the significance of the word "almost" in Hebrews 9:22?
12. Was it possible for a sin offering to be efficacious if it did not produce a heart realization, humility and contrition? Give scriptural evidence for your answer.
13. In what way was the Old Testament sacrificial system deficient?
14. Explain how the sacrifice of Christ opened up a better hope—or a new and living way to God.
15. When the Bible talks about an imperfect law and replacing the old system, is it referring to ceremonial law or moral law? Explain.
16. What biblical evidence do we have that crucifixion *facilitated*, rather than *caused* Jesus' death?
17. What does the Bible mean when it states that Jesus "bore our sins?"
18. Is there any evidence that profound emotional grief and heart trauma are related? How does this correspond with Isaiah 53:11–12?
19. What is the biblical evidence for and significance of Jesus' *premature* death on the cross?
20. Describe in detail how Christ's shed blood and substitutionary sufferings solved, once and for all, God's difficulties in reconciling man to Himself.

Chapter Six

1. How can a church sanctuary become an effective hiding place for sinners?
2. Can you be saved solely by repenting of sin? Can you be saved without repenting of sin?
3. Is the critical factor in salvation whether we accept

Christ, or whether or not He accepts us?

4. Does it matter to God at the point of salvation if we have unconfessed, unrepented sin in our hearts?

5. Is repentance a divine invitation or a divine commandment? Give supporting evidence for your answer.

6. Is repentance essentially a surrender, or a cure? Explain.

7. What do we indicate to God when we desire and determine to hold on to our sin?

8. Explain the steps involved in true repentance.

9. What is the difference between confession of sin and repentance?

10. What happens to us when we realize the truth about our sin, and yet decide to remain unchanged?

Chapter Seven

1. What is the basic distinction between intellectual faith and saving faith?

2. Why is saving faith regarded as virtuous?

3. Describe the elements of faith (substance and evidence) mentioned in Hebrews 11:1.

4. What is the difference between Christian faith and existentialism?

5. Is it possible to believe anything without evidence? Explain.

6. Why does "yo-yo" Christianity not measure up to the biblical definition of saving faith?

7. What is the role of the Holy Spirit in the process of coming to a saving faith?

8. Briefly define antinomianism. What is its error?

9. What do we learn from a thorough reading of James 2:14–26?

10. Are we saved by faith, or saved by grace?

Chapter Eight

1. Describe the basic aspects of any good, personal relationship.

2. What happens to a relationship when commitment is withdrawn?
3. What is wrong with the statement: "He lost his *fellowship* with the Lord, but not his *salvation*"?
4. Give a brief definition of the word *truth.*
5. Based on the scriptural evidence in this chapter, how would you define the "if" condition?
6. When Jesus came into the world He brought two equally significant messages—what were they?
7. What are the two potential sources of condemnation?
8. What is an "altar relationship"?
9. Briefly define *discipleship.* Why is biblical discipleship not legalistic?
10. Describe the process that takes place in the human heart when the rightful rulership of Christ is challenged.

Chapter Nine

1. What is the basic difference between *positional* and *experiential* sanctification?
2. What ultimately is the difference between a positionally sanctified, carnal Christian living for himself supremely and an unregenerate, natural man living for himself supremely?
3. Upon examining the I Corinthians 3:1–4 passage in context, what is the Apostle Paul actually stating? Do these verses establish a category for carnal Christians?
4. What are the two main aspects of the new covenant?
5. Give a brief definition of the word *sanctified.*
6. What does it mean to abide in Christ?
7. What is the difference between attempting to secure spiritual victory via abstinence as opposed to abiding in Christ?
8. Why are we afraid to let go of our lives? What does this reveal to us?
9. Why is it *not* a good idea to build our own cross?
10. What is the importance of spiritual vision and how is it to be obtained?

Chapter Ten

1. Why is it important to share objective truth as opposed to subjective experiences in our evangelism?
2. Give two reasons why every Christian needs to share the Gospel message with others.
3. Is compassion for the lost sufficient motive for preaching the Gospel? Explain.
4. What was Jesus really saying to Peter when He closed the book of John with the words "Feed My sheep"? Who do the sheep represent?
5. What is the danger of misunderstanding what it means to be "not of this world"? What is apocalyptic fatalism?
6. If we are going to conquer in this world with Christ, what three things do we need to allow Him to do? Explain in detail.
7. What was the basic message in Jesus' parable of the pounds?
8. Give your understanding of Proverbs 24:11.
9. Why are all non-Christ-centered revolutions doomed to fail?
10. What has proven to be the seed of the Church down through the centuries? Why?

FOOTNOTES

Chapter One

* A. W. Tozer, *The Knowledge of the Holy* (Harper & Row), p. 11.

* F. C. Happold quoted in *Christianity on Trial* (Tyndale), p. 111.

1. C. S. Lewis, *Surprised by Joy* (Harcourt, Brace & World), p. 231.

2. A. W. Tozer, *Of God and Men* (Christian Publications), p. 122

3. A. W. Tozer, *The Knowledge of the Holy* (Harper & Row), pp. 9,10,12.

4. A. W. Tozer, *God Tells the Man Who Cares* (Christian Publications), p. 47.

5. Arnold Lunn quoted in *Christianity on Trial* (Tyndale), p. 134.

6. C. S. Lewis, *The Problem of Pain* (Macmillan), p. 50.

7. Ibid, p. 51.

8. A. W. Tozer, *God Tells the Man Who Cares* (Christian Publications), p. 14.

9. C. S. Lewis, *Surprised by Joy* (Harcourt, Brace & World), pp. 220,221.

10. Elie Weisel, *Night* (Avon), p. 44.

11. If, then, it is true of the Latin (payment) doctrine of the Atonement in general that it is wholly comprehended within a rigid legal scheme, it is doubly true of the Protestant form of that doctrine. The thoroughness of the logical consistency with which the legal idea is carried through gives it a monumental character; the impression which it gives is that of a massive building in a

solid and austere style, capable of withstanding the storms of centuries.

Consult Gustaf Aulen, *Christus Victor* (Macmillan), p. 130.

12. C. S. Lewis, *Mere Christianity* (Macmillan), p. 136.

Chapter Two

* Duncan Campbell, *God's Standard* (Christian Literature Crusade), p. 50.

* Charles G. Finney, *Finney's Systematic Theology* (Bethany), p. 30.

1. Robert J. Ringer, *Looking Out for #1* (Fawcett Crest), p. 12.

Chapter Three

* Karl Menninger, *Whatever Became of Sin* (Hawthorn), p. 19.

1. Ibid., p. 19.

2. Gerald Dworkin, *Determinism, Free Will and Moral Responsibility* (Prentice-Hall), p. 1.

3. Karl Menninger, *Whatever Became of Sin* (Hawthorn), p. 13.

4. Hal Lindsay, *The Liberation of Planet Earth* (Zondervan), pp. 63,67.

5. Anna Russell quoted in *The Crisis in Psychiatry and Religion* (Von Nostrand), p. 49.

6. Augustine, *Marriage and Concupiscence* 2.15.

7. Ibid., 1.5,1.9,1.24,2.37,16,17 & *On Original Sin* 2.42.

8. Lewis Sperry Chafer, *Major Bible Themes* (Dunham Publishers), p. 136.

9. Hal Lindsay, *The Liberation of Planet Earth* (Zondervan), p. 49.

10. Gordon C. Olson, *Sharing Your Faith* (Bible Research Fellowship, Inc.).

11. Ibid., chap. 3, p. 4.

12. Lewis Sperry Chafer, *Major Bible Themes* (Dunham Publishers), p. 141.

13. Robert J. Ringer, *Looking Out for #1* (Fawcett Crest), p. 46.

14. C. S. Lewis, *The Problem of Pain* (Macmillan), pp. 55,57.
15. Original author of adaptation unknown. Quoted in *Whatever Became of Sin* (Hawthorn), pp. 11,12.
16. Ibid., p. 188.
17. Charles G. Finney, *The Guilt of Sin* (Kregel), p. 77.

Chapter Four

* Malcolm Muggeridge, *Jesus The Man Who Lives* (Fontana), p. 16.
* C. S. Lewis, *Mere Christianity* (Macmillan), p. 182.
1. Malcolm Muggeridge, *Jesus Rediscovered* (Family Library), p. 45.
2. Albert Barnes, *The Atonement* (Bethany Fellowship), p. 239.
3. P. P. Waldenstrom, *Be Ye Reconciled to God* (Men for Missions), p. 3.
4. Albert Barnes, *The Atonement* (Bethany Fellowship), p. 220–221.
5. Ibid., p. 220–221.
6. *Agapeland* (Candle Company Music)
7. Nathan Beman, *The Atonement In Its Relations to God and Man* (Newman–1844), p. 35.
8. Gustaf Aulen, *Christus Victor* (Macmillan), p. 58.
9. Robert J. Ringer, *Looking Out for #1* (Fawcett Crest), p. 46.
10. Ibid., p. 88.
11. C. S. Lewis, *Mere Christianity* (Macmillan), p. 182.

Chapter Five

* Charles G. Finney, *Finney's Systematic Theology* (Bethany Fellowship), p. 209.
* Gregory of Nazianzus, Quoted by Gustaf Aulen in *Christus Victor* (Macmillan), p. 58.
1. Malcolm Muggeridge, *Jesus Rediscovered* (Family Library), p. 50.
2. Gustaf Aulen, *Christus Victor* (Macmillan), p. 2.
3. Ibid., pp. 8,9.
4. Nathan S. Beman, *The Atonement In Its Relation to God And Man* (Newman–1844), pp. 94–95,106.

5. Caleb Burge, *An Essay On The Scripture Doctrine of Atonement* (Reprinted by Bible Research Fellowship), pp. 490–491.

6. C. S. Lewis, *Mere Christianity* (Macmillan), p. 179.

7. Colin Chapman, *Christianity on Trial* (Tyndale), pp. 489, 490.

8. Malcolm Muggeridge, *Jesus Rediscovered* (Family Library), pp. 20,21.

9. See also Psalm 94:21, Ezekiel 3:18, Matthew 27:24,25, Luke 11:50.

10. P. P. Waldenstrom, *The Christian Doctrine of the Atonement* (Covenant Press), p. 22.

11. James J. Lynch, *The Broken Heart* (Basic Books), pp. 11, 13,56,68.

12. Colin Parkes, *Bereavement: Studies of Grief in Adult Life* (International Universities Press—New York).

13. C. David Jenkins, "Psychologic & Social Precursors of Coronary Disease (First of Two Parts)" *New England Journal of Medicine* 282 (1971), pp. 244–254.

14. George L. Engel, "Sudden Rapid Death During Psychological Stress: Folklore or Folk Wisdom?" *Annals of Internal Medicine* (1971) pp. 771–782.

15. Pierre Barbet, *A Doctor At Calvary* (Image Books), p. 73.

16. Malcolm Muggeridge, *Jesus Rediscovered* (Family Library), pp. 53,56.

17. The Latin (Commercial Transaction) doctrine gives us a series of acts standing in relatively loose connection. The actual atonement consists in the offering of satisfaction by Christ and God's acceptance of it; with this act men have nothing to do except in so far as Christ stands as their representative. Justification is a second act, in which God transfers or imputes to men the merits of Christ; here, again, there is no direct relation between Christ and men. Next, we have sanctification, a third act with no organic connection with the preceding two.

See Gustaf Aulen, *Christus Victor* (Macmillan), p. 150.

Chapter Six

* C. S. Lewis, *The Problem of Pain* (Macmillan), p. 91.
* Alexander Solzhenitsyn, "Repentance and Self-Limitation," *From Under the Rubble* (Bantam), p. 107.
1. Webster's New World Dictionary (Collins & World).
2. Malcolm Muggeridge, *Jesus Rediscovered* (Family Library), p. 47.
3. C. S. Lewis, *The Problem of Pain* (Macmillan), p. 60.
4. Alexander Solzhenitsyn, "Repentance and Self-Limitation," *From Under the Rubble* (Bantam), p. 134.
5. C. S. Lewis, *The Problem of Pain* (Macmillan), p. 46.
6. Alexander Solzhenitsyn, "Repentance and Self-Limitation," *From Under the Rubble* (Bantam), p. 128.
7. Charles G. Finney, *True and False Repentance* (Kregel), p. 14.
8. Alexander Solzhenitsyn, "Repentance and Self-Limitation," *From Under the Rubble* (Bantam), p. 128.
9. See Luke 3:8, 19:8; Acts 26:20.

Chapter Seven

* Os Guiness, *The Dust of Death* (Inter-Varsity), p. 358.
* A. W. Tozer, *God Tells the Man Who Cares* (Christian Publications), p. 135.
* Andrew Murray (Source unknown).
1. Ambrose Bierce, *The·Devil's Dictionary.*
2. Os Guiness, *The Dust of Death* (Inter-Varsity), p. 358.
3. Vaughn, quoted in *Broken Bread* (Gospel Publishing House), p. 136.
4. John W. Follette, *Broken Bread* (Gospel Publishing House), p. 136.
5. C. S. Lewis, *Mere Christianity* (Macmillan), p. 123.
6. A. W. Tozer, *God Tells the Man Who Cares* (Christian Publications), p. 135.
7. Os Guiness, *The Dust of Death* (Inter-Varsity), pp. 336, 337.
8. Augustine, in his work "On the Gospel of St. John,"

stated, "seek not to understand that thou mayest believe, but believe that thou mayest understand." Although this statement has a catchy rhyme, it rests upon a faulty concept. That concept is that evidence is not an integral part of faith.

9. Francis Schaeffer, *He Is There and He Is Not Silent* (Hodder & Stoughton), pp. 95,96.

10. Simone Weil, quoted in *Jesus the Man Who Lives* (Fontana), p. 46.

11. Dietrich Bonhoeffer, *The Cost of Discipleship* (Macmillan), pp. 47,48.

Chapter Eight

* George MacDonald, quoted in *Mere Christianity* (Macmillan), p. 172.

* Dietrich Bonhoeffer, *The Cost of Discipleship* (Macmillan), p. 63.

1. J. F. Strombeck, *Shall Never Perish* (VanKampen Press), pp. 130–131.

2. Gordon C. Olson, *Sharing Your Faith*, Chart IX, p. 3 (Bible Research Fellowship).

3. Guy Duty, *If Ye Continue* (Bethany Fellowship), p. 12.

4. Ibid., p. 99.

5. Ibid., p. 99.

6. Dietrich Bonhoeffer, *The Cost of Discipleship* (Macmillan), pp. 88–92.

7. Elmer F. Suderman.

8. Charles G. Finney, *The Guilt of Sin* (Kregel), p. 79.

Chapter Nine

* A. W. Tozer, *Of God and Men* (Christian Publications), p. 63.

* Francois Fenelon, *Christian Perfection* (Harper & Row), p. 64.

1. Malcolm Muggeridge, *Jesus the Man Who Lives* (Fontana), p. 51.

2. Francis Schaeffer, *The Church Before the Watching World* (Inter-Varsity), p. 41.

3. Gordon Olson, *Sharing Your Faith* (Bible Research Fellowship), ch. 12, p. 1.
4. *Unger's Bible Dictionary* (Moody Press), p. 966.
5. *Scofield Reference Bible*, pp. 1213,1214.
6. Ernest C. Reisinger, *What Should We Think of the Carnal Christian?* (Banner of Truth Trust), p. 6.
7. Ibid., pp. 6,7.
8. *Unger's Bible Dictionary*, (Moody Press), p. 966.
9. Ernest C. Reisinger, *What Should We Think of the Carnal Christian?* (Banner of Truth Trust), p. 12.
10. Ibid., pp. 13,14.
11. Gordon Olson, *Sharing Your Faith*, (Bible Research Fellowship), ch. 12, p. 6.
12. Charles G. Finney, *Sanctification* (Christian Literature Crusade), p. 47.
13. Ibid.
14. Gordon Olson, *Sharing Your Faith* (Bible Research Fellowship), ch. 11, p. 9.
15. Ibid., ch. 12, pp. 4,6.
16. Charles G. Finney, *Sanctification* (Christian Literature Crusade), p. 46.
17. Watchman Nee, *Love Not the World* (Christian Literature Crusade), pp. 40,41.
18. Malcolm Muggeridge, *Jesus Rediscovered* (Tyndale), pp. 45,46.
19. C. S. Lewis, *Mere Christianity* (Macmillan), p. 167.
20. John W. Follette, *Broken Bread* (Gospel Publishing House), p. 183.
21. Fenelon, *Christian Perfection* (Harper & Row), pp. 83, 84.
22. John W. Follette, *Broken Bread* (Gospel Publishing House), p. 70.

Chapter Ten

* Robert Hall Glover, *The Biblical Basis for Missions* (Moody Press), p. 34.
1. Samuel M. Zwemer, (Introduction) *The Biblical Basis for Missions* (Moody Press).

244

2. Evgeny Barabanov, "The Schism Between the Church & The World," *From Under the Rubble* (Bantam), p. 186.
3. Ibid., p. 187.
4. Ibid., p. 188.
5. Ibid., p. 181.
6. "Concerning Religious Societies"—Resolution of the Central Committee, April 8, 1929, Para. 17.
7. "Desolation Row" by Bob Dylan (Highway 61 Revisited), Columbia Records.
8. Malcolm Muggeridge, *Jesus Rediscovered* (Pyramid Publications), p. 159.
9. Alvin Toffler, *Future Shock* (Bantam Books), p. 220.
10. Malcolm Muggeridge, *Jesus Rediscovered* (Pyramid Publications), p. 159.
11. Leonard Ravenhill, *Sodom Had No Bible* (Ravenhill Books), p. 77.
12. Alexander Solzhenitsyn, "The Abuse of Freedom" *(U.S. News & World Report)*, September. 13, 1976.
13. Alexander Solzhenitsyn, *The Gulag Archipelago Pt. I* (Harper & Row), p. 178.
14. Alexander Solzhenitsyn, (Forward) *From Under the Rubble* (Bantam Books).
15. J. Osward Sanders, *Spiritual Leadership* (Lakeland), p. 89.

*Source of quotations beginning each chapter.